## ALL ABOUT

# HOUSE WIRING

**FLOYD MIX,** *President*
**Goodheart-Willcox Co., Inc.**

**HOMEWOOD, ILL.**
**THE GOODHEART-WILLCOX CO., INC.**
*Publishers*

# Introduction

Each time you turn on a light or start an appliance, you buy and use electricity. Electricity is brought to your home by power lines which are maintained by the utility company serving your community.

You and you alone are responsible for how well electricity serves you after it reaches your home.

Electrical Living -- a goal desired by all of us -- starts with Adequate Wiring.

An Adequate Wiring Installation Provides:

1. Enough branch circuits of large enough wire to conduct a full measure of electrical energy to your lights and appliances.

2. Enough outlets and switches to provide for convenient and efficient use of lights and appliances.

The purpose of this book is to take the "mystery" out of house wiring. It tells how to determine what wiring is needed. It describes in easy-to-understand language, how to install wiring in both new and existing residences; wiring capable of serving SAFELY the lighting, appliances and equipment of Today, as well as those of Tomorrow.

# Contents

# ALL ABOUT HOUSE WIRING

# Getting Started in House Wiring

In the design of an electrical system for the home, two basic factors must be kept in mind. One factor is SAFETY and the other PROVIDING A SYSTEM THAT WILL PERMIT FULL AND CONVENIENT USE OF ELECTRICAL EQUIPMENT now being used and which may be procured in the future.

Instructions in ALL ABOUT HOUSE WIRING will apply to wiring of new, single-family dwellings, individual dwelling units of multi-family residences, and to electrical modernization of existing residences.

## SOME ELECTRICAL TERMS YOU SHOULD KNOW

It is easy to understand the terms VOLTS, AMPERES AND WATTS, if we compare the flow of electricity through a wire to water flowing through a pipe. Neither electricity nor water will flow unless there is pressure back of it.

## VOLTS

Water pressure is measured by pounds; electric pressure by VOLTS.

9

## AMPERES

In measuring the amount of water passing through a pipe, the term gallons is used. In electricity the unit of measurement is AMPERES.

## WATTS

Watts is the unit of measurement that tells us how much electricity is being used. It is determined by multiplying the amperes by the volts.

KILOWATT: 1,000 watts.

KILOWATT-HOUR (KWH): 1,000 watts used for one hour.

## CIRCUIT

A wire provided for electricity to follow from the point of supply to the electric appliance and back.

## RESISTANCE

Electrical friction, or the tendency of the wire to keep the electric current from passing through it.

## OHMS

The unit of measurement of electrical resistance. We speak of ohms of resistance in electricity like we would pounds of pull necessary to break a certain line, were we to discuss fishing lines.

## SWITCH

A device for controlling a circuit or some of its parts.

## HORSEPOWER: One horsepower (HP) equals 746 watts.

## POLARIZING

Identifying wires throughout the system by color to help assure that "hot" wires will be connected only to "hot" wires and that "neutral" wires run in continuous uninterrupted circuits back to the ground terminals.

## DIFFERENCE BETWEEN ALTERNATING CURRENT (a.c.) AND DIRECT CURRENT (d.c.)

Direct current flows only in one direction and is the type delivered by all batteries. In alternating current the voltage is applied in one direction one instant and the other the next. In other words, the direction of flow reverses continually. Each two reversals is called a cycle, (short interval of time between each change of direction when there is neither voltage nor current). The number of cycles per second is called frequency. Most residential wiring today is a.c. 60-cycle frequency. Check with your Utility Company if in doubt.

## NATIONAL ELECTRIC CODE

The National Electric Code is a set of rules approved by the National Board of Fire Underwriters which serves as a guide to providing safety in wiring. All house wiring should be installed in accordance with the National Electric Code and existing municipal and state codes or regulations applicable to the work. Requirements of the local utility company should also be met.

When wiring a building, adding an outlet, or replacing a switch or receptacle only Underwriters' approved parts and devices should be used. The Underwriters Laboratories, supported by manufacturers, insurance companies and other interested parties, test the quality of electrical parts and devices to see if they meet certain minimum standards.

Their stamp of approval on a switch, fixture, or roll of wire is your assurance of safety, but does not necessarily indicate that two approved pieces are of equal quality.

All materials and wiring, including lighting fixtures, should be installed in a workmanlike manner. Even high-quality merchandise may be unsafe if it is carelessly or improperly installed.

# *Wiring Materials and Devices*

## WIRE SIZES

Actual sizes of copper conductors (electrical wires) without insulation are shown in Fig. A-1. The sizes shown are in American Wire Gauge (AWG), which is the same as the Brown and Sharpe Gauge (B&S).

Some properties of copper conductors are shown in Fig. A-2.

## INSULATION

Fig. A-3, lists various types of insulation, together

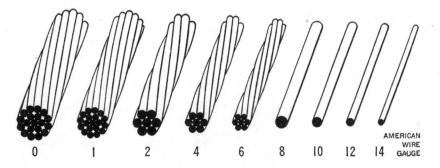

0    1    2    4    6    8    10    12    14    AMERICAN WIRE GAUGE

A-1.    Actual diameters of sizes of copper conductors.

with the "type-letter" which is the identification accepted by the trade in referring to the particular grade of insulation, the maximum allowable operating temperature, and the purpose for which wiring with various types of insulation is best suited.

| Size of Conductor AWG | Ohms Per 1000 Feet 25°C--77°F Bare Conductor | Bare Conductor Diameter--Inches | No. of Wires |
|---|---|---|---|
| 14 | 2:575 | .064 | Solid |
| 12 | 1.619 | .081 | Solid |
| 10 | 1.018 | .102 | Solid |
| 8 | .641 | .129 | Solid |
| 6 | .410 | .184 | 7 |
| 4 | .259 | .232 | 7 |
| 2 | .162 | .292 | 7 |
| 1 | .129 | .332 | 19 |
| 0 | .102 | .373 | 19 |

A-2.    Properties of copper conductors.

| Insulation | Type Letter | Maximum Operating Temperature | Suitable For |
|---|---|---|---|
| Code Rubber..................... | R | 60°C (140°F) | General Use |
| Moisture-Resistant Rubber......... | RW | 60°C (140°F) | General Use and Wet Locations |
| Latex Rubber..................... | RU | 60°C (140°F) | General Use |
| Moisture-Resistant Latex Rubber.. | RUW | 60°C (140°F) | General Use and Wet Locations |
| Heat-Resistant Rubber............. | RH | 75°C (167°F) | General Use |
| Thermoplastic.................... | T | 60°C (140°F) | General Use |
| Moisture-Resistant Thermoplastic.. | TW | 60°C (140°F) | General Use and Wet Locations |
| Weatherproof..................... | WP | 80°C (176°F) | Open Wiring by Special Permission |

A-3.    Insulation table.

If a given type of conductor insulation is subjected for any considerable length of time, to a temperature higher than its maximum operating temperature, the insulation will deteriorate rapidly.

The conductors of an electrical system should be of sufficient size so that not only the development of dangerous temperatures is prevented, but also wasted power in the form of voltage drop is restricted. It is impractical to avoid all voltage drop, but it must be held to nominal, practical proportions.

CABLES

Cable used in house wiring consists of two or more insulated wires, grouped together in an overall cover-

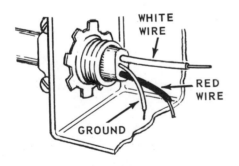

A-4. Plastic sheathed cable, as shown here, may be used to provide continuous grounded system.

ing. Cables with both non-metallic and flexible metal covering, Figures A-4 and A-5, are used extensively in residence wiring. Cable which is not waterproof should be used only for indoor wiring.

LEAD SHEATHED CABLE: In lead-sheathed cable, rubber-covered wires have an overall lead covering to

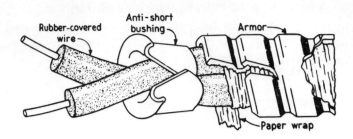

A-5.   Flexible steel armored cable.

protect them from moisture and elements in the soil. Such cable is made especially for laying underground. The lead sheath is easily damaged by mechanical means and should be protected by placing it in galvanized conduit.

PLASTIC SHEATHED CABLE:  A cable consisting of two or more insulated wires with a flexible plastic protective covering. This may be used either indoors or out, and is approved for direct burial in the earth as it has high resistance to damage by corrosion, moisture and rodents. It should be laid underground 2 ft. or more... deep enough to avoid injury by shovels, plows, etc.

LAMP OR FIXTURE CORDS:  Flexible cords used to connect lamps, irons, radios, etc., to outlets. Lamp cord wire is made up of fine strands to give it flexibility. It is then covered with rubber insulation and a cotton or rayon wrapping.

For heating appliances, electric irons. waffle irons, etc., a special cord known as heater cord is required. This has a layer of asbestos wrapped

16

around each rubber-covered wire and an overall layer of cotton or rayon braid.

## CONDUIT

Conduit (pipe for protecting electrical wiring) is used extensively in wiring of new buildings and to some extent on parts of modernizing jobs where more than

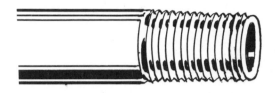

A-6.    Rigid conduit.

average protection for the wiring is needed. Conduit comes in two different types, rigid conduit and thin-wall conduit or tubing.

RIGID CONDUIT: Rigid conduit, Fig. A-6, may be either black or galvanized and looks very much like water pipe; the principal differences being that the conduit is softer, making it easier to bend, and is inspected closer for sharp projections on the inside that might cut the insulation from wires when pulling them through the conduit.

Rigid conduit comes in the same sizes as water pipe, 1/2 inch, 3/4 inch, 1 inch, $1\frac{1}{4}$ inch and larger. It may be cut and threaded with the same tools used for water pipe.

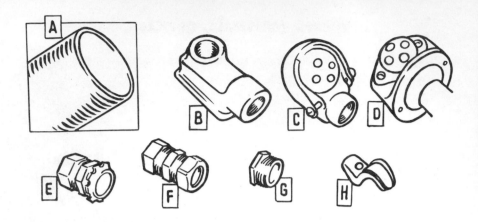

A-7. (a) Thin-wall conduit. (b) Entrance L used to turn conduit into building. (c) Entrance head. (d) Flanged entrance head. (e) Connector for attaching conduit to box. (f) Coupling for joining ends of conduit. (g) Adapter for attaching conduit to threaded fittings. (h) Strap for fastening conduit to wall.

THIN-WALL CONDUIT: Thin wall conduit (EMT-Electrical Metallic Tubing) is made in galvanized finish only and may be used either indoors or out. The inside measurement is the same as rigid conduit, but the wall is thin making the outside measurement less. The wall is so thin that it cannot be threaded, so special pressure fittings are used to couple joints together and to connect the conduit to switch and outlet boxes. See Fig. A-7.

OUTLET BOXES

Outlet boxes come in three principal shapes -- octagon, square and round, Fig. A-8.

The octagon (eight sided) box is most commonly used. It comes in 3 1/4 and 4-inch sizes and may be obtained with clamps for attaching either non-metallic or armored cable. For most work, the larger box is preferable as it holds more wires and provides extra space for working.

Round boxes are seldom used except as shallow ceiling boxes. Ordinary cable clamps or conduit cannot be properly fastened to the sides, so special cable clamps must be used.

With a blank cover an outlet box is used as a junction box (where wires are joined); with a surface switch it is used as a switch box; with a duplex receptacle cover it is used as a convenience outlet box

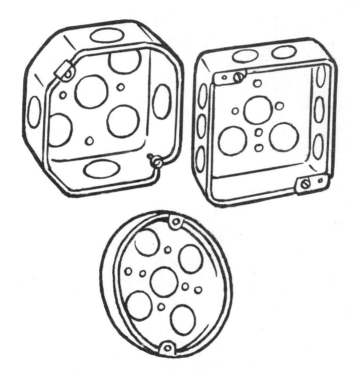

A-8. Outlet boxes come in three shapes: Octagon, Square, Round. Each has 1/2 inch diameter knockouts for connecting conduit or cable.

(place to plug in a lamp or appliance); with a rosette cover it is used as a drop-cord box; with a key or keyless porcelain receptacle or a fixture and canopy it is used as a fixture box.

SWITCH BOXES

According to the Code, all switches and receptacles except those of the surface type, must be installed in switch boxes. Refer to Fig. A-9.

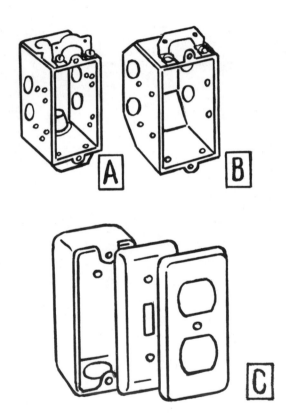

A-9.   Switch and receptacle boxes.
(a) Box with clamps for armored cable.
(b) Beveled corner box.
(c) Surface mounted utility box which screws to wall surface, with switch and
      duplex receptacle covers.

A-10.   Single-pole toggle switch.

Switch boxes commonly come in 2 1/4 and 2 1/2 inch depths, but depths of 1 1/2 to 3 1/2 inches are available. They may be obtained either with or without special cable clamps.

## NON-METALLIC BOXES

Non-metallic switch and outlet boxes, made of porcelain or bakelite, are available for use in damp basements or outbuildings. They are non-corrosive and shockproof. Although breakable,they will stand ordinary use. Such boxes are not approved by all codes, so be sure to check with local authorities before using them.

## SWITCHES

SINGLE-POLE TOGGLE SWITCH: This switch, as shown in Fig. A-10, is the type most commonly used in house wiring today. Single pole toggle switches have two terminal screws (places where wires are attached) and are used to make and break the electrical circuit; usually a circuit controlling only one light or appliance.

A-11.

DOUBLE-POLE SWITCH: A double-pole switch controls two lights, like basement light, and a head-of-the-stairs pilot light. See Fig. A-11.

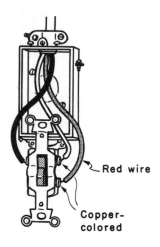

A-12.  Three-way switch.

THREE-WAY SWITCHES: Three-way switches are used to control lights from two locations, Fig. A-12. Two three-way switches are required for each installation.

FOUR-WAY SWITCHES: These are used when we want to control an electrical circuit from three or more points. When using four-way switches, it is necessary to use two three-way switches in the circuit and to install a four-way switch between the three-way switches.

OIL BURNER SWITCH: Some cities require installation of a special switch near the head of the basement stairs for controlling the oil burner if an emergency arises. A single-pole switch is ordinarily

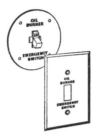

A-13. Oil burner switches.

used, the only difference between this and any other installation being that the switch plate is finished in red and lettered to indicate the purpose for which the switch is intended. See **Fig. A-13.**

A-14. Door switch which operates when door is opened and closed.

DOOR SWITCH: The use of a door switch, Fig. A-14, furnishes a desirable way to provide automatic control of closet lighting.

A-15.    Switch and convenience outlet.

SWITCH AND CONVENIENCE OUTLET COMBINA-TION: Used for locations where it is desirable to combine switch control with a convenience outlet, Fig. A-15.

A-16.    Night light with two switches.

NIGHT LIGHT: In a night light such as shown in Fig. A-16, one switch controls the night light; the other switch is used to control hall or room lighting.

MERCURY SWITCH: In a mercury switch the switching operation is completely silent. The switch handle tips a sealed tube partially filled with mercury to make and break the circuit.

Mercury switches are desirable for childrens' rooms, bathrooms, etc., where the click of the ordinary switch is annoying.

DELAYED-ACTION SWITCH: Another modern type of switch is the delayed-action switch. This holds the light on long enough for you to get out of the room before it turns off.

## CONVENIENCE OUTLETS

Outlet receptacles most commonly used are of the duplex type as shown in Fig. A-17. Each receptacle has

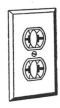

A-17.    Duplex outlet receptacles.

A-18. Grounding-type outlet--three wire. Designed for grounding exposed metal parts of portable appliances. In metallic wiring systems, the ground is made directly through the conduit or metal cable. For non-metallic systems, the ground is completed by using a third wire which serves as a grounding conductor.

two terminal screws on each side; one pair for connecting the receptacle to the line, and another which may be used for wires leading to an additional light or device in the circuit.

Drawings A-18 to A-27 inclusive, illustrate a variety of other outlet receptacles and lamp holders with which those interested in handling complete wiring jobs should become familiar.

A-19. Grounding type outlet for providing ground contact on three-wire 115/230 volt circuit.

A-20. Weatherproof duplex convenience outlet. When not in use, covers which are attached to plate by bead chains, may be used to prevent exposure to moisture.

A-21. Clock hanger. Recessed to provide convenient nesting of surplus cord.

A-22. Fan hanger. Yoke mounting with "T" slot outlet and .060 inch brass plate. Permits secure positioning of fan, the weight being supported by the box, with no strain on the outlet or plate.

A-23. Telephone outlet.

A-24. Porcelain lampholder--keyless. Provided with shade holder groove.

A-25. Porcelain lampholder with pull chain.

A-26. Box mounting for garage, farm buildings, etc.

A-27. Range outlet and cord set. Used to connect range to outlet.

## FUSES AND CIRCUIT BREAKERS

Fuses and circuit breakers act as "safety valves" for the wiring system. They protect electrical wiring from damage due to overload and short circuit.

FUSES: Fuses as shown in Fig. A-28, contain strips of easy-to-melt metal through which the current

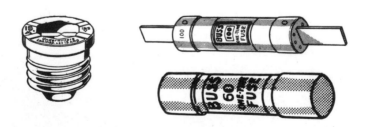

A-28. Left. Common fuse plug. Right. Cartridge-type fuses.

must pass. A fuse "blows" when the flow of current is more than the metal strip can carry. The metal strip melts and the circuit opens. Screw-type fuses come in capacities up to 30 amperes. Fuses of 60 to 100 amperes are of the cartridge type.

FUSTATS: Fustats, Fig. A-29, are protective devices somewhat similar to common plug fuses. They also protect appliances and circuits from high currents or continuous overloads. A fustat is made so a small

A-29. Left. Fustat. Right. Fustat adapter.

block of solder melts when heated by a continuous overload of high current. After the solder has melted, a spring attached to the fuse strip pulls the circuit open.

With each different size of fustat, a different adapter is used. The adapter is screwed into a plug fuse socket. The adapter is constructed so that when it is once placed in the socket, it locks in place and cannot be removed. This prevents inserting fuses that are too large.

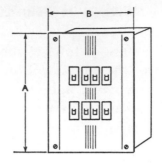

| No. of circuits (single pole) | A (height) | B (width) |
|:---:|:---:|:---:|
| 2 | 9″ | 6″ |
| 4 | 9″ | 8″ |
| 8 | 14″ | 9″ |
| 16 | 15″ | 14″ |

A-30. Above, left. One type of thermal magnetic (individual breaker) circuit breaker. Individual breakers are grouped in box, under cover as shown at right. The assembly consists of given number of breakers of fixed rating--containing from two up to 16 single-pole positions.

CIRCUIT BREAKERS: A circuit breaker provides another means of protecting an electrical circuit from damage caused by overload and short circuits. It too, has an alloy metal strip through which the current passes. However, instead of melting when the current is too high, the metal strip opens the circuit. When the cause of the breaker opening is corrected, the breaker may be reset and the circuit closed. See Fig. A-30.

CIRCUIT BREAKERS THAT SCREW INTO FUSE SOCKETS: Also available for protecting electrical wiring circuits are miniature circuit breakers that screw into fuse sockets. The protector trips on dangerous overloads. Service is restored by pressing a small button that protrudes from the top.

## VISIT LOCAL ELECTRIC SHOPS

Illustrations and descriptions on the preceding pages will give you an idea of what is available in standard electric wiring materials and devices.

Many other items of practical value are also available, and it is suggested that you visit electric-supply stores and shops in your locality and become familiar with items available from these stores, before planning any house wiring job.

## TOOLS YOU WILL NEED

In residential wiring, tools you will need include:

HAMMER: For driving nails, staples, fastening hangers.

BIT OR DRILL: Long-shank electrician's bit 5/8 in. size, for boring wood or soft metal.

BIT BRACE: For use with drill; also screwdriver.

KEYHOLE SAW: For cutting openings for switches, outlet boxes, etc.

HACK SAW: For cutting metallic cable, various other cutting jobs.

TEST LIGHT: To trace circuits, check fuses, etc.

BLOW TORCH OR ELECTRIC SOLDERING IRON: For soldering wire splices, connections.

FOLDING RULE: 6-foot, for measuring openings, wire lengths.

CHISEL: Wood for notching joists, studs, flooring.

PIPE WRENCHES: For working with rigid conduit. Lever-jaw wrenches may be used as pipe wrench substitutes.

LINEMEN'S PLIERS: For cutting wire, gripping locknuts.

LONG NOSE PLIERS: For making splices, forming eyes for connecting wires to terminal screws.

POCKET KNIFE: For cleaning wires, removing insulation.

FISH WIRE: For pulling wire through wall openings and conduit.

CONDUIT BENDER: Very necessary when bending conduit.

SCREWDRIVERS: To tighten screws, locknuts, etc.

REAMER OR ROUND FILE: Tapered, for removing burrs from ends of rigid conduit.

# *Splices, Connections*

In making splices and connections in electrical wiring these rules should be followed:

1. Make splices and connections as strong as wires that have not been spliced.

2. Solder all connections to make them secure and provide good electrical contact.

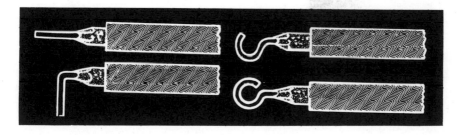

B-1.   Forming eye on end of wire.

3. Insulation should be replaced so it is equal to that of the original insulation.

## FORMING EYES FOR TERMINAL SCREW CONNECTIONS

When fastening a wire to a switch or receptacle, an

eye or hook should be made on the end of the wire to provide ample contact between the surface of the wire, the screw and the base, Fig. B-1.

The procedure to follow is:

1. Remove 1/2 to 3/4 inch of insulation. Use a knife to pare away the insulation in the same manner as you would to sharpen a pencil. Be careful not to damage the wire. If linemen's pliers are available, the wire can be inserted through the handle side of the pliers next to the jaw and insulation broken by pressing on the handles of the pliers.

2. Clean wire by carefully scraping off the insulation.

3. Make right angle bend in wire, and use long nose pliers to draw the end around to form an eye.

Note that the wire is turned clockwise. When placed under a screw head it pulls tighter as the screw is tightened.

## MAKING COMMON SPLICE

A common or Western Union splice is shown in Fig. B-2.

The procedure in making this splice is:

1. Remove about three inches of insulation from the ends of both wires.

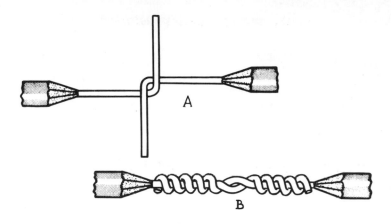

B-2.   Making common splice.

2. Clean wires by scraping with knife.

3. Using pliers, make a right angle bend on each wire, detail A. Fig. B-2.

4. Hold wires together tightly with pliers at joint. With second pair of pliers wrap loose ends to form a finished splice as shown in detail B.

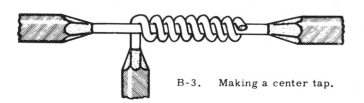

B-3.   Making a center tap.

## CENTER OR T-TAP

The center tap, Fig. B-3, is used where it is necessary to attach an additional wire to a continuous wire.

Procedure:

1. Remove about 1 1/4 inches of insulation from main wire.

2. Remove about 1 1/2 inches of insulation from wire to be attached.

3. Clean both wires by scraping with a knife.

4. Splice wires as shown in the drawing, Fig. B-3.

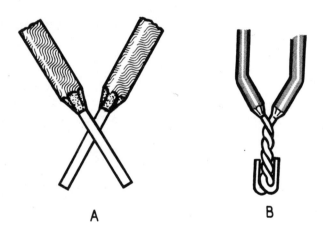

A          B

B-4.    Pigtail splice.

## PIGTAIL SPLICE

The pigtail splice, Fig. B-4, is used in outlet boxes for attaching fixture leads, or other places where there is no pull on the wires.

## SPLICES, CONNECTIONS

Procedure:

1. Remove about 1 1/2 inches of insulation from the ends of the wires to be spliced.

2. Clean wires by scraping with knife.

3. Using linemen's pliers, twist wires together and bend over the ends as shown in detail B, Fig. B-4.

B-5. Using solderless connector. Wire ends are cleaned, and twisted together. Connector is screwed on until no bare wire shows.

## SOLDERLESS CONNECTORS

The drawing, B-5, shows a solderless connector which is used principally for attaching fixture leads. In using such a connector, the ends of the wires to be joined are inserted into the connector which is then twisted clockwise to hold the wires together tightly.

## END TAP

This splice, Fig. B-6, is used to connect a small

feeder to a larger wire, or to several wires previously joined together with a pigtail splice.

Procedure:

1. Remove about 1 1/4 inches of insulation from end of larger wire and about two inches from end of small wire.

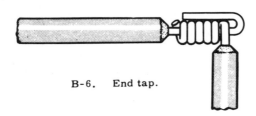

B-6.    End tap.

2. Clean wires by scraping with knife.

3. Starting from middle of large wire, wrap smaller wire as shown in B-6; then clamp larger wire over small wire.

## SOLDERING SPLICES

Soldering of splices is a very important part of a good wiring job. If electricity is available, an electric soldering iron can be used to good advantage. If not, a blowtorch may be used to heat the soldering coppers.

Steps to be followed:

1. Thoroughly clean the wires to be soldered.

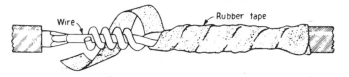

B-7.    Applying rubber tape to spliced wires.

2. If wire solder with flux core is used, be sure it is rosin-core type. Acid-core solder has tendency to corrode, weaken the splice and cause poor electrical contact.

3. If bar solder or solid wire solder is used, flux of proper type should be applied to surfaces to be soldered. Flux prevents forming of oxides which keep solder from sticking.

4. Soldering copper may be reconditioned by: First cleaning with file. Next, the copper must be tinned. Heat copper, rub on block of sal ammoniac while still hot, then coat with solder.

5. Use soldering copper to heat wires to be spliced until they will melt the solder.

6. Apply enough solder to fill space between wires and to give entire joint a thin, even coating.

Warning: Excess solder that may drop off wires is hot. Be careful.

TAPING SPLICES

In taping splices both rubber tape and friction tape should be used. See Fig. B-7. The rubber tape which should be applied first, serves as the primary insulator. Each layer of tape should overlap the preceding layer by about one-half the width of the tape.

To do a good job, make the rubber tape overlap the insulation on the wire, stretch the tape a bit, then wind it round and round over the exposed joint.

Next, apply friction or plastic tape. This acts both as a binder for the rubber tape and as additional insulation. Wrap the second covering of tape tightly over the rubber tape, letting each layer overlap the preceding layer as described for rubber tape.

Friction tape should not be used without rubber tape because it has a tendency to loosen with age.

# Installing Outlet, Switch Boxes, Conduits, Cables

## OUTLET AND SWITCH BOXES

Information on quantity of outlets needed and where they should be placed, room by room, to provide adequate wiring for a modern residence, will be found on page 129. Information on circuit requirements is given in the Service Requirements Section, page 51.

On a house wiring job, the first step, after the locations of the outlet boxes have been decided, is to install the outlet and switch boxes.

In some cases wood bridging strips between studs are used for box supports. Fastening a box directly to a stud, and using a metal support are shown in Fig. C-1. The mounting ears on the ends of the boxes are adjustable to compensate for materials of various thicknesses. In making an installation the ears should be adjusted so the front edge of the box is flush with the wall surface. Boxes for convenience outlets are usually placed 10 to 12 inches above the floor and boxes for switches 40 to 50 inches above floor level. Height to install other outlet boxes depends on the purpose for which the outlets are to be used.

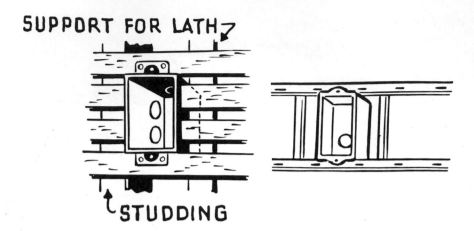

SUPPORT FOR LATH

STUDDING

C-1. Installing outlet boxes. Left. Box is nailed to stud in wall. Right. Metal support is used to hold box between studs.

Knockouts as required to take the number of conduits or cables needed should be removed before fastening the boxes in place. The boxes in position will serve as direction guides for the running of the conduit or cable.

## INSTALLING CONDUIT AND CABLE

Conduit, both the rigid and thin-wall types, should be properly installed and attached to switch or outlet boxes before any wires are inserted. The wires are then pushed in at one end of the conduit and if more than about 10 feet long, pulled from the other using a fish tape, and connections made in the boxes. Applying talcum powder to the insulated wires will make them easier to pull through the conduit. Notching of joists and supporting members should be kept to a minimum.

On new construction, where the finish floor is laid

on furring strips instead of directly on the subfloor, there is space for conduit between the floors.

## BENDS ALLOWED

In using both rigid and thin-wall conduit, the Code specifies that not over four quarter bends are allowed

C-2.    Left.  Bender for rigid conduit.  Right.  Bender for thin-wall conduit.
Both benders have the handles removed.

in a run of conduit (distance from box to box). Conduit should be supported with pipe straps placed not more than $4\frac{1}{2}$ feet apart.

## RIGID CONDUIT IS THREADED

Rigid conduit is threaded on the ends and is joined together like water pipe. Cutting of the conduit can best be done using a fine-tooth (32 per inch) hacksaw blade.

The end of the pipe should be smoothed and burrs which might scrape insulation off the wire removed by using a tapered reamer or a round file. Threading of the pipe may be done with pipe dies such as used in threading water pipe.

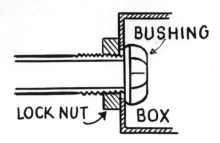

C-3.    Section view of rigid conduit attached to outlet box.

Long, easy bends in rigid conduit may be made without bending tools. For shorter bends, a conduit bender as shown in Fig. C-2, is desirable.

Fig. C-3 shows how rigid conduit is fastened to an outlet or switch box.

Connector                           Coupling

C-4.    Special fittings for thin-wall conduit.

## THIN-WALL CONDUIT

Thin-wall conduit is too thin to thread; special fittings, such as shown in Fig. C-4, are used for coupling lengths together and connecting it to outlet and switch boxes.

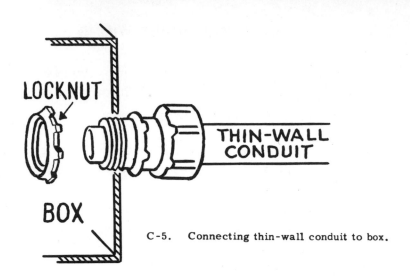

LOCKNUT

THIN-WALL CONDUIT

BOX

C-5.    Connecting thin-wall conduit to box.

In bending thin-wall conduit a bending tool, such as shown in Fig. C-2, is used. A smooth, even bend is made by taking short bites; the shorter the bite, the better the bend. A little experimenting with a bending tool will quickly enable you to get the knack of using it.

Pipe straps should be used to support thin-wall conduit; straps to be spaced not more than $4\frac{1}{2}$ feet apart.

Fig. C-5, shows how thin-wall conduit is connected to a box.

## INSTALLING ARMORED AND SHEATHED (NON-METALLIC) CABLES

Both armored metal and non-metallic sheathed cables may be used for exposed or concealed work in ceilings, floors and walls. Both are suitable for use in wiring new residences and in modernizing wiring in existing residences.

Such cables are particularly appropriate for modernizing jobs as they can be run through hollow spaces in walls with less difficulty.

Both armored and sheathed cable should be fastened up by using straps, Fig. C-6, as needed to support

C-6.    Left. Strap for supporting conduit. Right. Conduit clamp.

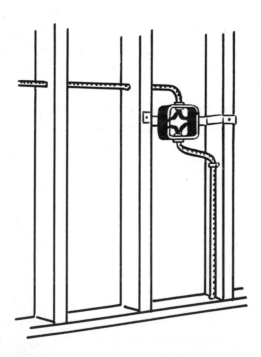

C-7.    Typical installation of cable. Note how cable is fastened and that it runs through holes bored in center of the studs.

the cable - one at least every $4\frac{1}{2}$ feet when run on the surface and within 12 inches of every outlet or switch box. Supports may be omitted in finished walls, In using cable straps, care must be taken not to crush or mar the cable.

When placed at right angles to studs or joists, both armored and sheathed cables should be run through bored holes, Fig. C-7, or placed on a running board, or between guard strips for protection. All cable wiring must have outlet, junction or switch boxes at both ends of every run, and all cable joints or splices must be made inside boxes.

Guard strips or conduit should be provided as needed to protect non-metallic cable from mechanical injury. Cable passing through the floor should be protected at least six inches above the floor using pipe or conduit.

## CUTTING ARMORED CABLE

The metal covering of armored cable may be cut with a fine-tooth hacksaw. Be sure to see to it that the saw does not cut into the insulation on the wires. Another way of cutting the metal armor is to bend it to a sharp angle and then use a pair of heavy tin snips to do the cutting. In either case, the short piece of armor which has been cut loose, may be easily pulled off the end of the wires. Sharp points left when cutting the cable should be trimmed away and the edges filed smooth.

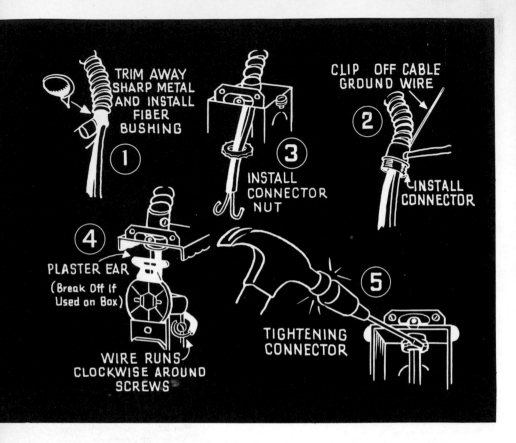

TRIM AWAY SHARP METAL AND INSTALL FIBER BUSHING

① 

③ INSTALL CONNECTOR NUT

CLIP OFF CABLE GROUND WIRE

② INSTALL CONNECTOR

④ PLASTER EAR (Break Off If Used on Box)

WIRE RUNS CLOCKWISE AROUND SCREWS

⑤ TIGHTENING CONNECTOR

C-8.    Step-by-step procedure in connecting armored cable to outlet box, using separate connector.  Some boxes have built-in cable clamps.  Connectors come as straight, 45-degree and 90-degree connectors.

Insulation on wires inside the armor may be removed with a pocket knife.

Connecting an armored cable to an outlet box is shown in Fig. C-8. Sheathed cable is connected the same way; the clamp must be of the proper size to fit the sheathed cable. A bushing of tough fiber is inserted between the wires and armored cable to keep the metal from cutting into the insulation on the wires. Be sure to screw the connectors tight and drive the connector nuts solidly home within the boxes. In connecting armored cable to a distribution panel cabinet, care should be taken to see that the cabinet is grounded; otherwise a separate ground wire is needed.

Lengths of armored cable up to 25 feet may be installed without ground connections provided the cable is at least seven feet above the floor and there is no chance of the cable coming into contact with something that is grounded.

KNOB AND TUBE WIRING

The practice of using single, rubber-covered wires supported by porcelain insulators (knobs, tubes, cleats) is considered obsolete and is not recommended for modern residential wiring jobs. For this reason knob and tube wiring will not be covered in this book.

PLUG-IN MOLDING

The use of plug-in molding -- steel channel or raceway above the baseboard to carry electrical wiring, which is suitable for both new wiring and modernization of existing systems, will be found on page 123.

# Service Requirements

Electrical service provided for today's modern home should be 115-230 volts. This means that both 115 and 230 volt current will be available.

Three wires are required. One wire will be neutral or a ground wire; the other two will be "hot" wires. There will be 230 volts of electric pressure

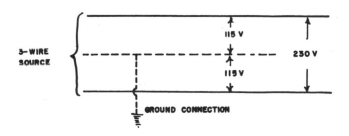

D-1.   A 230-volt circuit is a combination of two 115-volt circuits.

between the two hot wires and half that, or 115 volts, between the neutral or grounded wire, and either of the hot wires. See Fig. D-1.

## SERVICE ENTRANCE EQUIPMENT

Service entrance wires are connected to the main switch and fuse, or main circuit breaker. This service

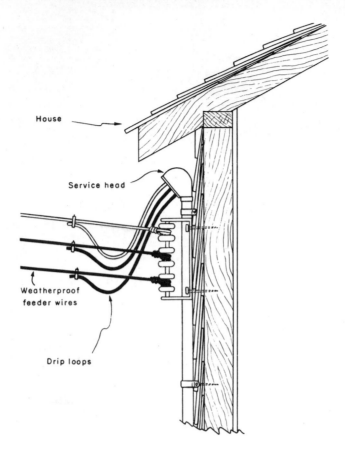

House

Service head

Weatherproof
feeder wires

Drip loops

D-2.  Typical service entrance installation.

entrance equipment serves as the junction point from which electricity is dispatched to various parts of the house, Figs. D-2, and D-4.

For homes up to 3,000 square feet in floor area, the rating of the service equipment should be a minimum of 100 amperes. For larger homes, also homes using electricity extensively for air conditioning, heating, etc. a larger service will be required. See Fig. D-3.

# SERVICE REQUIREMENTS

| Nominal Rating | Maximum Capacity | Main Switch | Main Control Center Units | Size of Service Wire | Size of Conduit | Utilization Circuits |
|---|---|---|---|---|---|---|
| 100A | 24,000 watts | 100A Sw. or 100A Cir. Bkr. | 2-50A 1-20A (Water Heater) | 2 — No. 2 1 — No. 4 | 1 ¼ | General Purpose Electric Cooking Electric Laundry Water Heater Air Conditioning |
| 150A | 36,000 watts | 200A Sw. (150A Fuses) or 150A Cir. Bkr. | 3-50A 1-20A (Water Heater) | 2 — No. 2/0 1 — No. 2 | 2" | General Purpose Electric Cooking Electric Laundry Air Conditioning Water Heater Electric Heating (Small Homes) |
| 200A | 48,000 watts | 200A Sw. (200A Fuses) or 200A Cir. Bkr. | 4-50A 1-20A (Water Heater) | 2 — No. 4/0 1 — No. 2/0 | 2" | General Purpose Electric Cooking Electric Laundry Air Conditioning Water Heater Electric Heating (Temperate Climate) |

D-3.  Table showing recommended capacities of service entrance conductors for various loads.

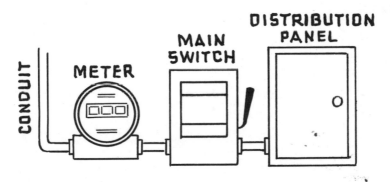

D-4.  Meter, main switch and distribution panel installation.

The drawing D-4 shows a typical meter, main switch and distribution panel installation.

Hooking up the three incoming wires in a typical 230-volt system, including a range, water heater and four branch circuits, is shown in Fig. D-5. The dis-

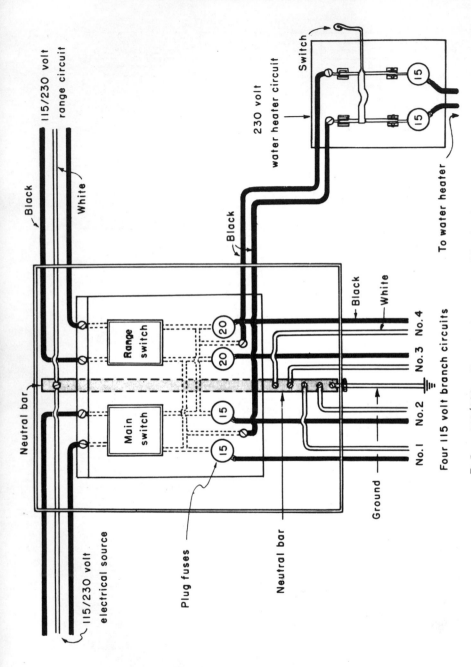

D-5.  115/230 volt control center and feeder layout.

tribution panel to be installed should always be large enough to provide for two or three spare circuits.

Cartridge-type fuses in the main switch blocks conduct the current to the individual circuit fuses. In a 230-volt line both hot wires are fused. Fuses are not used in neutral or ground wires.

## GROUND IS NECESSARY

Residential electrical systems should be grounded to limit the voltage to within that for which they are designed. A typical ground installation is shown in Fig. D-6. A special ground clamp is used to make the connection to the water pipe. In the pipe line the water meter should be "bridged" or shunted to keep the ground path continuous, even if the water meter is removed.

## DETERMINING NUMBER OF CIRCUITS NEEDED

The initial cost of installing electrical circuits in a home is such a small percentage of the total cost of the building, (usually less than 3 per cent) that it is penny-wise and pound foolish to install minimum requirements.

Over a period of time the more efficient and effective operation will offset the slight additional investment.

The recommendations for determining the number of circuits needed for average residential use which

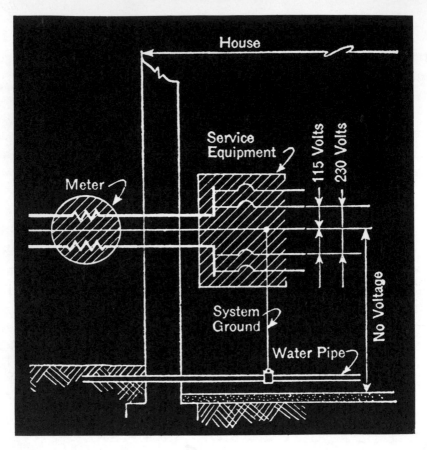

D-6. Electrical wiring layout showing neutral conductor being grounded to a water pipe.

follow, are those of the Industry Committee on Interior Wiring Design.

## GENERAL PURPOSE CIRCUITS

General purpose circuits shall supply all lighting outlets (permanent fixture installations) throughout the house and all convenience outlets (outlets into which are plugged floor lamps, small appliances, etc.) except the convenience outlets in the dining room, breakfast room, kitchen, pantry and laundry.

These circuits shall be provided on the basis of one circuit for not more than 500 square feet of floor area. Outlets supplied by these circuits shall be divided equally among the circuits.

General purpose circuits shall be protected by using 15 ampere fuses. No. 14 wire is the minimum allowed by the wiring Code. No. 12 wire is more satisfactory and is recommended for all general purpose circuits.

## APPLIANCE CIRCUITS

Two 20-ampere circuits are recommended for the convenience outlets in the kitchen, pantry, breakfast room, dining room and laundry, in a residence having a floor area of 1,500 square feet or less.

The wiring for such circuits to be so installed that outlets supplied from both circuits are available in both the kitchen and the laundry. For residences with a floor area greater than 1,500 square feet, one 20-ampere circuit for the convenience outlets in the kitchen, pantry, breakfast room and dining room; one 20-ampere circuit for the convenience outlets in the laundry; and one 20-ampere circuit supplying convenience outlets in both the kitchen and the laundry.

The number of 20-ampere circuits specified are necessary because more and more appliances of high wattage, with automatic features are being used that make possible the performance of several household tasks simultaneously.

The use of three-wire circuits for supplying convenience outlets in the locations mentioned, is suggested as an economical means for dividing the load and offering practical operating advantages.

In dividing the 230-volt current into two 115-volt branches, it is advisable to keep the load balanced between the two circuits as evenly as possible.

## SIZE CONDUIT NEEDED

The size conduit to use (rigid or thin-wall) depends on the size and number of wires to be inserted into the conduit. According to the Code, the maximum number of wires allowed in each size conduit is as follows:

| Size of wire | Number of wires allowed when conduit is | | |
| --- | --- | --- | --- |
| | 1/2 in. | 3/4 in. | 1 in. |
| 14 | 4 | 6 | 9 |
| 12 | 3 | 5 | 8 |

## NUMBER OF WIRES IN BOXES

The following table gives the maximum number of conductors, not counting fixture wires, allowed by the Code in various size boxes where no switch, cable clamp or fixture stud is included:

| Size of box | No. 14 wire | No. 12 wire |
|---|---|---|
| $1\frac{1}{2}$ x $3\frac{1}{4}$ in. octagon | 5 | 5 |
| $1\frac{1}{2}$ x 4 in. octagon | 8 | 7 |
| $1\frac{1}{2}$ x 4 in. square | 11 | 9 |
| $1\frac{3}{4}$ x $2\frac{3}{4}$ x 2 switch | 5 | 4 |
| $1\frac{3}{4}$ x $2\frac{3}{4}$ x $2\frac{1}{2}$ switch | 6 | 6 |
| $1\frac{3}{4}$ x $2\frac{3}{4}$ x 3 switch | 7 | 7 |

For each switch or receptacle mounted in a box, deduct one wire.

## INDIVIDUAL EQUIPMENT CIRCUITS

Individual circuits shall be provided for the following equipment:

| Item | Capacity |
|---|---|
| Range (up to 12KW) | 35A-3W (35 ampere, 3 wire) 115/230V |
| Range (above 12KW) | 50A-3W - 115/230V |
| Fuel Fired Heating Equipment | (if installed - 15 or 20A-115V) |
| Dishwasher-Waste Disposer | (if necessary plumbing is installed) 20A-2W-115V |
| Water Heater | Consult local utility |
| Automatic Washer | 20A-2W-115V |

Consideration should also be given to adding circuits for the following household devices. The table should not be construed to list all equipment that might be desirable.

| Item | Circuit |
|---|---|
| Clothes Dryer . . . . . . . . . . . | .25A-3W-115/230V |
| Summer Cooling Fan . . . . . . . | .20A-2W-115 (Switched) |
| Air Cooling Unit . . . . . . . . . . | .25A-2W-230V |
| Home Freezing Unit. . . . . . . . | .20A-2W-115V or 230V |
| Water Pump (where used) . . . . | .20A-2W-115V or 230V |
| Bathroom Heater . . . . . . . . . | .20A-2W-115V or 230V |
| Work Shop or Bench (Power Tools). . . . . . . . . . | .20A-2W-115V |

In some instances one of the circuits may serve two devices which are not ordinarily used at the same time, such as a summer cooling fan and a bathroom heater.

The majority of appliances for residential use are made for 115-volt circuits. There is, however, a growing tendency to make fixed appliances for use on 230-volt circuits. It is recommended that the higher voltage be used in cases where a choice exists.

EXTRA CONTROL CENTERS

A trend in modern wiring worthy of consideration is placing control-centers near "the centers of load". This is covered in detail on page 152.

# Installing Switches, Outlets

## COLOR MARKING OF WIRES

In interior wiring the color code for branch circuits is:

Two wire circuit - one black and one white wire
Three wire circuit - one black, one white, one red
   (or two black and one white)
Four wire circuit - one black, one white, one red,
   one blue
Five wire circuit - one black, one white, one red,
   one blue, one yellow

The neutral or ground wire, which is white, should not be fused or switched, and should lead uninterrupted to every place in all circuits where 115-volt current is to be used.

## EXTRA WIRE AT BOXES

The wire should be pulled through the outlet box far enough so a minimum of six inches of wire will be left protruding. This amount is needed for making splices and connections.

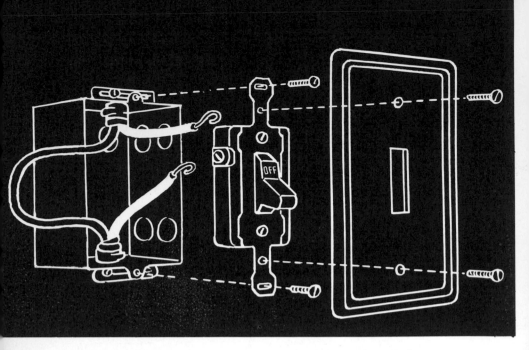

E-1.    Installing single-pole toggle switch.

## ATTACH WIRES TO PROPER TERMINALS

It is important not only to use the proper color wires for the "hot" and ground wires but to attach each to the proper terminal screws on the lamp or device. Terminal screws for the hot line are brass or copper colored; those for the ground wire are light or nickel colored.

A lamp is properly connected when the hot line is attached to the center pole and the grounded line to the screw shell of the socket.

WIRING SINGLE-POLE SWITCH

To add a switch to a common lighting circuit, simply cut the black or hot wire, and attach both ends to the terminal screws to the switch, Fig. E-1.

In cases where the wiring to the lamp is not accessible for installing a switch and it is necessary to detour the hot wire to the switch a piece of two-wire non-metallic or armored cable may be used to make the connection to the switch. In using a cable in this manner

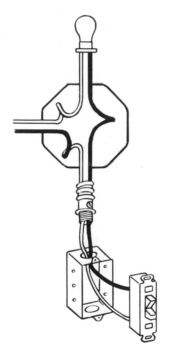

E-2.    Using piece of two-wire cable in connecting single-pole toggle switch.

it is necessary to use both the black and the white wires as hot wires. This particular use of a white wire as a hot wire is approved by the Code. The black wire should run from the switch to the light. See Fig. E-2.

WIRING THREE-WAY SWITCHES

Three-way switches are used to control a light from two different locations, such as a light at the head of a stairway, from both the foot of the stairway and the head. See Fig. E-3.

Three-way switches have three terminals. A simple explanation of the principle involved in a three-way switch circuit is given in Fig. E-4. Note that the circuit is completed when both switches are either up or down. The knife switches are intended only to show the

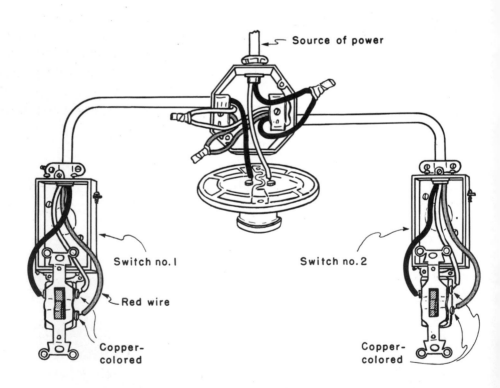

E-3.  Wiring diagram for three-way switch.

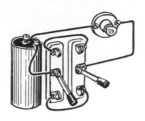

E-4. How three-way switch works. Note that the circuit is completed by moving both switches either up or down.

## INSTALLING SWITCHES, OUTLETS

principle involved and should not be used on a house wiring installation.

A four-way switch is installed between two three-way switches to control a light from more than two locations, Fig. E-5. A four-way switch has four terminals and is attached in the two wires running between two three-way switches.

In hooking up a switch with a pilot light the connection from the light to the switch (hot line) is made in the usual way, then an extra wire is run from the terminal of the switch to the pilot light. A neutral wire must also be provided to the pilot light, to complete the circuit.

OTHER CIRCUITS

Additional wiring diagrams will be found on pages 167 to 174 inclusive.

PROVIDING MASTER SWITCH CONTROL

Another feature of modern-day electrical wiring worthy of consideration is a master control of certain

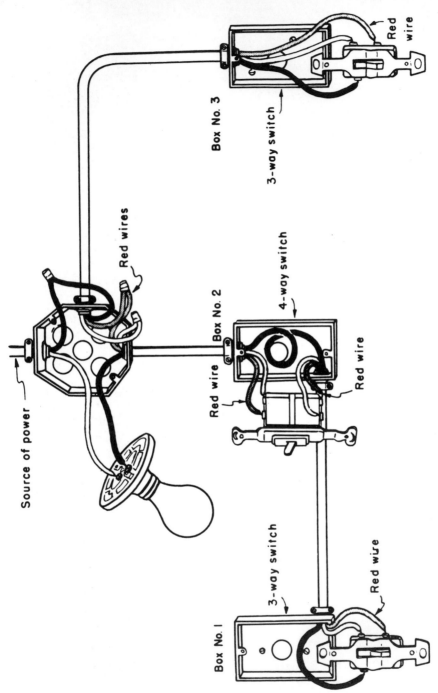

Source of power

Red wires

Red wire    Box No. 2

Red wire

Box No. 3

3-way switch

4-way switch

3-way switch

Red wire

Box No. I

Red wire

Red wire

E-5.    Diagram showing how an electric light may be controlled from three points, using one four-way and two three-way switches.

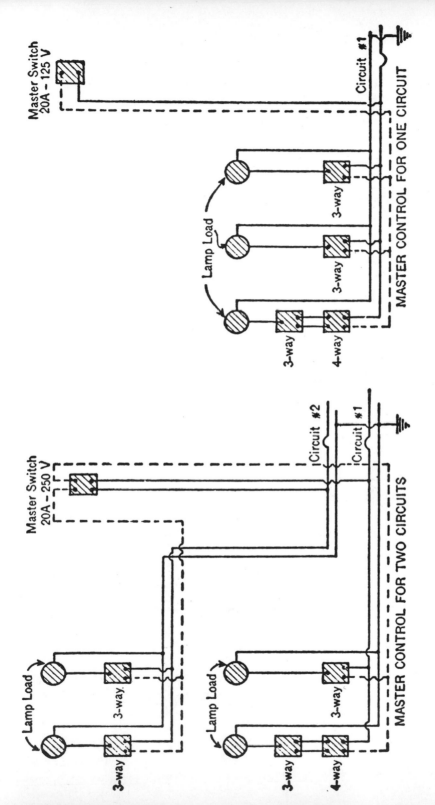

Master Switch
20A - 125 V

Circuit #1

Lamp Load

3-way

3-way

3-way

3-way

4-way

MASTER CONTROL FOR ONE CIRCUIT

Master Switch
20A - 250 V

Circuit #2

Circuit #1

Lamp Load

3-way.

3-way

Lamp Load

3-way

3-way

4-way

MASTER CONTROL FOR TWO CIRCUITS

E-6.    Master switch control wiring.

outlets from the owner's bedroom or other location. By using a master switch it is possible to turn on lights located at points inside or outside the house, independent of local switch controls.

More specifically, when the master switch is in the "off" position, the outlets under its control may be controlled by local switches. When the master switch is in the "on" position, the outlets under its control will all be "on" regardless of whether the local switches are on or off.

A master switch control wiring diagram is given in Fig. E-6.

## SERIES AND PARALLEL WIRING

Fig. E-7 shows the difference between series and parallel wiring. In series wiring the electricity to operate the second lamp must pass through the first,

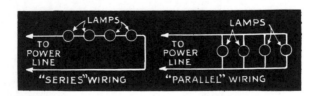

E-7.   Series and parallel wiring.

and so on. Series wiring is used when it is desirable to operate several low-voltage lamps off a line of higher voltage.

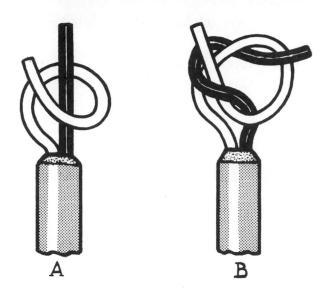

E-8.   Steps in typing an Underwriter's knot.

## INSTALLING BRASS LIGHT SOCKET

The procedure to follow in installing a brass light socket, Fig. E-8, E-9 and E-10:

First, take the socket apart. Bring the cord through the cap and anchor it by tying an Underwriters knot. This relieves stress on the terminal screws caused by weight of fixture and turning light on and off.

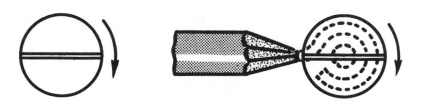

E-9.   Fastening end of wire to terminal screw.

Remove about three inches of the outside, or primary insulation from the end of each cord. Next, remove about 1/2 inch of the secondary insulation

E-10. Pull-apart and assembled views of brass shell socket.

from each wire, being careful not to cut any of the small wires. Finish the job by fastening the ends of the wires securely under the terminal screws, Fig. E-9.

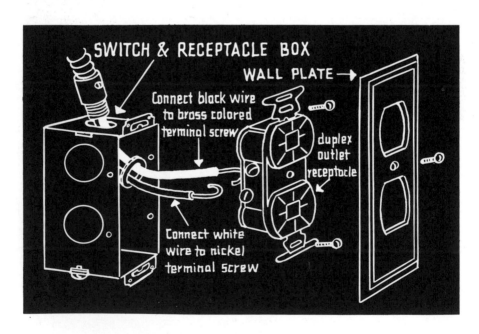

SWITCH & RECEPTACLE BOX

WALL PLATE →

Connect black wire to brass colored terminal screw

duplex outlet receptacle

Connect white wire to nickel terminal screw

E-11. Exploded view of convenience outlet installation.

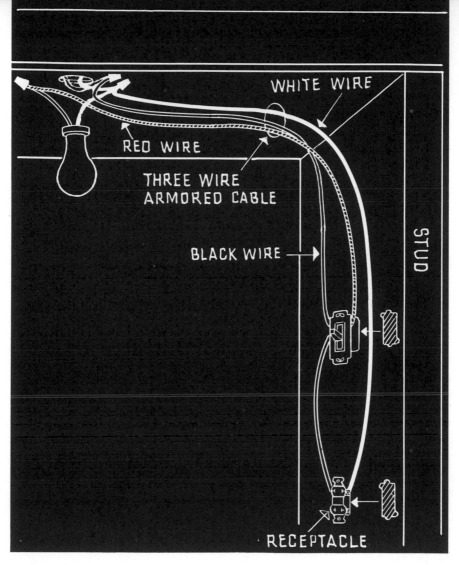

WHITE WIRE

RED WIRE

THREE WIRE
ARMORED CABLE

BLACK WIRE →

STUD

RECEPTACLE

E-12. Switch-receptacle hookup. On a regular wiring installation, three-wire cable would be used and wiring for the lamp, switch and receptacle would be installed in metal boxes.

## OUTLET INSTALLATION

Installation of a convenience outlet is shown in Fig. E-11. The hot (black) wire is connected to the brass colored terminal screw and the neutral or white wire is connected to the nickel colored screw.

Some boxes used for outlets and terminals have detachable sides. This permits ganging or assembling two or more boxes together. One-piece, twin and triple cover plates are available.

## NO-SHOCK OUTLETS

Accidental shocks, burns and short circuits caused by small children inserting hairpins, nails, scissors, etc., into current-carrying parts of electrical outlets can be prevented by using safety outlets. Such outlets have covers or caps which snap shut automatically when the plug is withdrawn. A number of types are available.

## SWITCH AND RECEPTACLE COMBINATION

Fig. E-12 shows a combination switch-receptacle wiring installation. If the receptacle is to be "hot" all the time, it must be attached to the hot line ahead of the switch.

# *Built-In Lighting*

## CORNICE LIGHTING

Cornice lighting creates inviting atmosphere in a room by accenting colorful wallpaper, beauty of

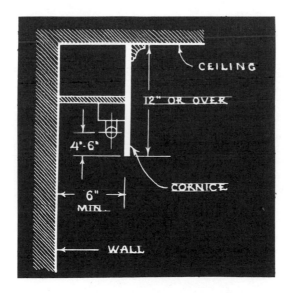

F-1.   Cornice lighting installation.

furniture and decorations. Fig. F-1 shows typical cornice lighting installations.

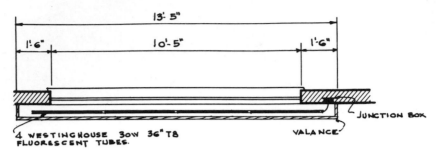

## Top View

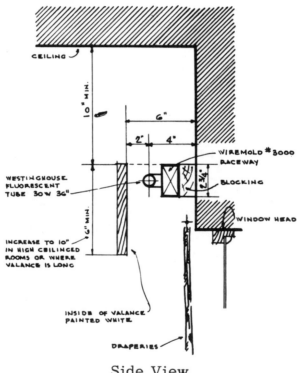

## Side View

F-2.   Typical installation of valance lighting at large window.

The light sources may be either incandescent or fluorescent. If incandescent, a combination of lumiline lamps may be used with sockets mounted back to back (to avoid shadows). Inside-frosted lumilines come in 40 and 60-watt sizes. The 40-watt size is one inch in diameter, 12 inches in length including the sockets; the 60-watt size is one inch diameter, 18 inches in length including the sockets.

Size and shape of lamps available make lumilines practical for cornice lighting. However, they produce greater heat and consume about four times as much electricity as fluorescent lamps, to provide the same amount of light.

IF FLUORESCENT: A combination of lengths may be used to fill the required space. Wherever possible use the same diameter of tubes: 3/4 inch, 1 inch or 1 1/2 inch. Lengths of fluorescent tubes including sockets are:

14-watt . . . . . . . . . . . . 15 inch length
15-watt . . . . . . . . . . . 18 inch length
20-watt . . . . . . . . . . . 24 inch length
25-watt . . . . . . . . . . . 33 inch length
30-watt . . . . . . . . . . . 36 inch length
40-watt . . . . . . . . . . . 48 inch length

Wall colors and the color of fluorescent tubes should be co-ordinated, the choice depending on whether a "cool" or "warm" atmosphere is desired.

Information on installation of wiring, switches, etc., given elsewhere in this book, is applicable to built-in lighting.

CORNICE BOARDS: Cornice boards may be made of 3/4 inch wood and should conform and harmonize with architectural and decorative elements in the room. The outside face may be painted, papered, covered with fabric, upholstered or left in natural wood finish. The inside should be given two or three coats of flat white paint, the wiring channel also being white.

Electrical wiring procedure as described in this book, should be followed in making the electrical installation.

## VALANCE LIGHTING

With valance lighting, windows and adjoining wall areas can be utilized as both useful and decorative means of reflecting artificial lighting. The color and texture of draperies are enhanced by the highlighting of fabric folds.

Valance lighting may be direct (down) or indirect (to the ceiling) or both. For indirect lighting, the top of the valance board should be 10 to 12 inches below the ceiling to allow light to spread out over the ceiling and avoid excessive ceiling brightness above the valance.

For direct lighting, the light source should be as high as possible in the valance and at least four inches out from the wall. Hang curtains and draperies close to the wall so light is in front of them.

Valances may be constructed of wood and painted or covered with decorative materials. See Fig. F-2.

## COVE LIGHTING

Cove lighting, Fig. F-3, provides pleasant indirect illumination from fluorescent tubes concealed by molding of wood, metal or plastic, designed to reflect structural or design elements of the room.

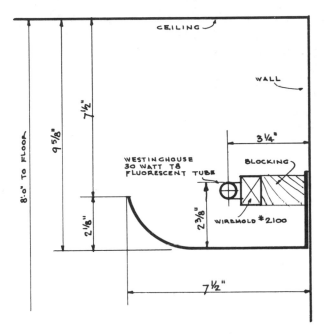

F-3.    Cove lighting detail.

Recessed coves provide more even illumination over entire ceilings. Coves in homes are not ordinarily used on walls over 18 feet apart. Rough or swirl plaster on ceilings should always be avoided. Matte papers or paints of high reflectance should be used on wall above coves and on ceilings. Interior of cove should be white for maximum efficiency. If height of room permits, light source should be 10 to 12

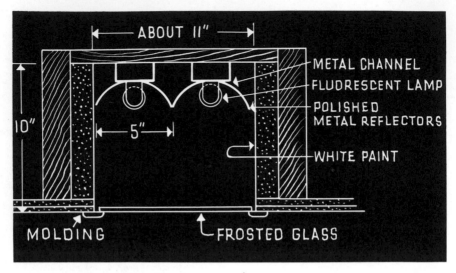

F-4.    Cross-section of soffit-lighting installation.

inches below the ceiling to insure good distribution of light.

## RECESSED LIGHTING

Recessed lighting may be used entirely for decorative effect, or it may be used to provide illumination over dining room table, steps, foyer, etc.

Recessed fixtures are available in various sizes. Long fixtures should be run parallel with the joists.

## SOFFIT LIGHTING

Soffit lighting is a tailored-to-the-job installation. In a kitchen it may be recessed into furring above a kitchen sink; in other rooms, within the overhead structure or alcove providing space for a bed, davenport, etc.

A typical soffit installation is shown in Fig. F-4. Installing two rows of lamps with polished metal directive reflectors, is recommended.

## WIREMOLD RACEWAYS

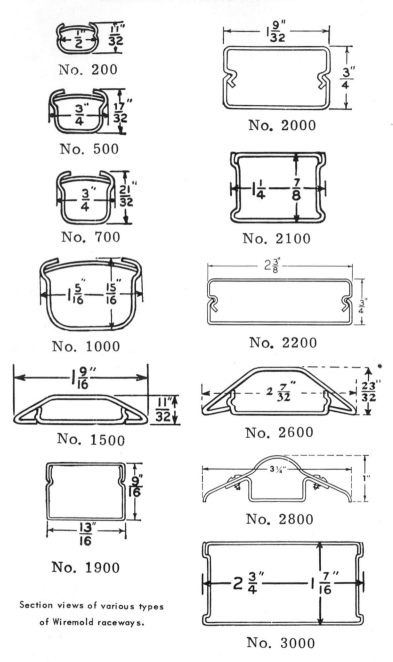

No. 200

No. 500

No. 700

No. 1000

No. 1500

No. 1900

No. 2000

No. 2100

No. 2200

No. 2600

No. 2800

No. 3000

Section views of various types
of Wiremold raceways.

# *Remote Control Systems*

## HOW REMOTE CONTROL SYSTEM WORKS

Take an ordinary single-pole switch and put a

thick iron cap over the handle like this then place

an electromagnet (the coil from a bell, for example)

over the metal-capped handle and now connect

wires from the coil to a battery through a push-button.

If this push-button is placed at a distance from the

switch, the circuit looks like this:

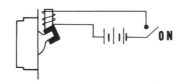

When the button is pushed the coil is energized and the
metal-capped handle is attracted to the coil. The
switch now is ON and will stay ON even though the

push-button is released. By placing a second coil under
the handle and connecting it to the same battery through
another push button it then becomes possible to shut the
switch OFF like this:

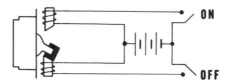

or the wiring can be simplified as follows:

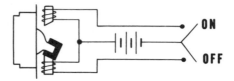

This is the fundamental principle of a remote-control
wiring system.

To show how these principles are applied in remote-
control wiring system, just two simple substitutions
are necessary (1) a transformer, similar to that used
for a door chime, is substituted for the battery, and
(2) a small two-coil relay is used in place of the
switch with the metal-capped handle and double electromagnet. The circuit then is:

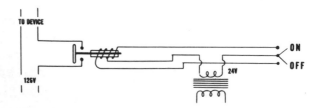

Obviously, there would be no point in putting this relay-switch where a single-pole switch is normally located. An appropriate place is right in the outlet box or sectional switch box to be controlled. This reduces the 115-volt lines. Since the switches are momentary contact devices, any number can be connected in parallel for multipoint control. Here is a set-up showing three switches and one relay.

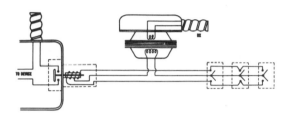

This is the basic circuit as used in all the remote-control wiring circuits.

## ·USING REMOTE-CONTROL SYSTEM IN RESIDENCE WIRING

The remote-control system of wiring provides a simplified way of controlling lights in every room in the house, plus the garage, basement, etc., from the master bedroom, or any desired location. It may be used to provide other conveniences and time-savers such as: turning off radio from telephone or television, turning on front entrance light from kitchen, controlling attic ventilating fan from various locations, turning on breakfast coffee from bedside (bedroom switch controls wall outlet in kitchen), etc.

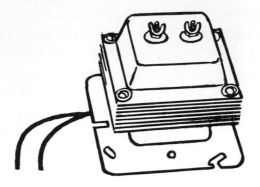

G-1.   Transformer (24-volt) used to operate relays in remote-control system.

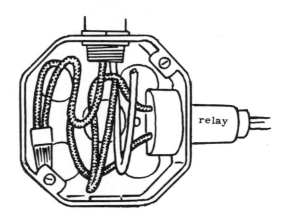

G-2.    Remote-control relay mounted in outlet box.

Definite ON and OFF positions of remote-control switches eliminate the need for checking whether a light is ON or OFF (basement playroom, for example) as must be done with conventional-type three or four-way switches.

The General Electric Remote Control System, which is featured in this book, uses a low-voltage (24-

volt) transformer to operate the remote-control relays. The transformer, Fig. G-1, has a rated output of 35 volt-amperes. The average residence will require only one transformer, regardless of the number of remote-control relays installed.

Switching of the 115-volt (tungsten filament and fluorescent lamp) circuit is accomplished by using relays which are actually small two-coil, solenoid-operated switches. These may be installed in the outlet box of the lighting fixture, or in pull boxes for the gang-mounted relay method of wiring. The barrel of the relay is inserted through a 1/2 inch knockout from the inside of the box. Thus, the 115-volt switch end remains within the box and the low-voltage end is outside. See Fig. G-2.

When one coil is momentarily energized with current from the transformer, the solenoid plunger moves, closing the 115-volt switch contacts. When the other coil is so energized, the solenoid opens this 115-volt switch. No current flows in the low-voltage circuit except for the brief length of time used to make the change in the 115-volt switching.

Pigtail leads of No. 14 wire are used for the 115-volt connections and pigtail leads of smaller wire are used for the low-voltage end to facilitate installation. The low-voltage leads are white, red and black for terminal identification.

Remote-control switches are available in two types -- one for flush mounting and the other for surface mounting. Both use the same switch mechanism, which is a single-pole, double-throw, momentary-

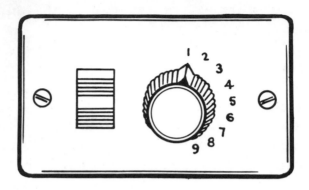

G-3.    Remote-control, master-selector switch.

contact, normally-open push-button type switch rated at three amperes, 24 volts, a.c.

A master control switch, Fig. G-3, is used, when it is desirable to control a number of circuits from a single location.

INSTALLATION PROCEDURE

Installation of remote-control systems should conform with requirements of the National Electrical Code, municipal and state codes and the requirements of the local electric utility company.

It is advisable to split the house plan into convenience zones, each containing approximately equal number of relays, Fig. G-4.

Use two-conductor remote-control wire (No. 20

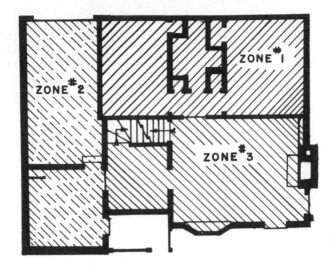

G-4.    Floor plan of home divided into convenient remote-control zones for transformer loops.

wire with 1/64 inch insulation) for transformer cir-cuits; one circuit for each zone. It is important to connect all identified or ribbed conductors from the separated circuits to the same transformer terminal.

Use three-conductor remote-control wire for all runs from individual switches to relay locations. The wires may be run from individual switches to the relay locations, or, wires may be run from switch to switch and finally to the relay location. To prevent possibility of poor connections all connections should be soldered.

When installing the low-voltage wiring the use of a stapling gun, designed for remote-control wire greatly speeds the job. If a stapling gun is not used, insulated staples are suggested. It is important to allow at least 12 inches of wire at the end of each run for making connections. This provides a safety margin for

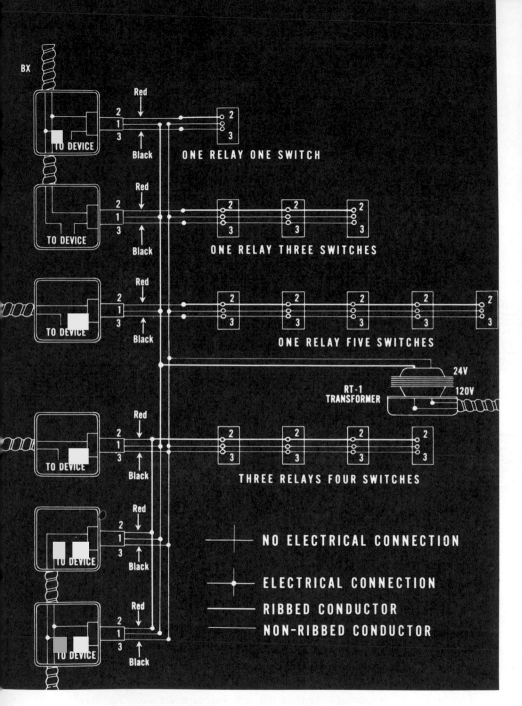

BX

Red
2
1
3
TO DEVICE
Black
ONE RELAY ONE SWITCH

Red
2
1
3
TO DEVICE
Black
ONE RELAY THREE SWITCHES

Red
2
1
3
TO DEVICE
Black
ONE RELAY FIVE SWITCHES

RT-1
TRANSFORMER
24V
120V

Red
2
1
3
TO DEVICE
Black
THREE RELAYS FOUR SWITCHES

Red
2
1
3
TO DEVICE
Black

NO ELECTRICAL CONNECTION

Red
2
1
3
TO DEVICE
Black

ELECTRICAL CONNECTION
RIBBED CONDUCTOR
NON-RIBBED CONDUCTOR

G-5.    Remote control circuits.

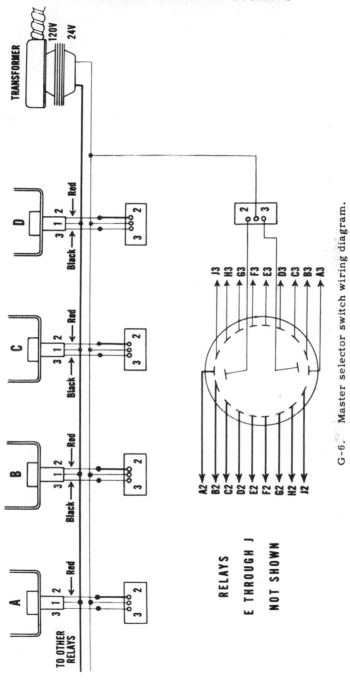

G-6. Master selector switch wiring diagram.

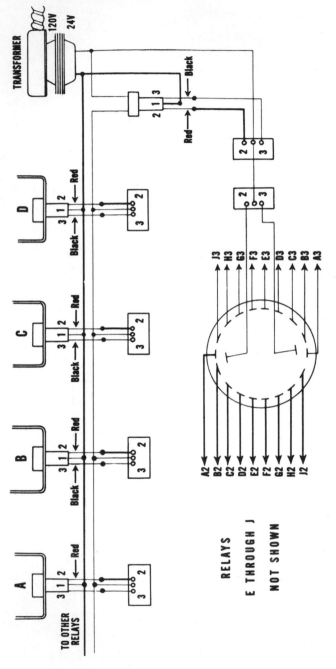

G-7. Master selector switch with lock-out circuit.

changing switch connections and permits the formation of the necessary loop when the relay is inserted in the knockout.

See wiring circuits and switch diagrams, Figs. G-5, G-6, G-7.

## ROUGHING-IN STAGE, ZONE-GROUPED OR GANG-MOUNTED RELAY METHOD

1. Rough in service and run branch circuits to uncontrolled outlets in the conventional manner. Install outlet boxes.

2. Run one or more branch circuits to each of the gang box locations. Mount gang boxes.

3. Mount outlet boxes at fixture locations. Run 115-volt wiring from gang boxes to each controlled outlet box.

4. Mount switch supports at all switch locations.

5. Mount transformer near one of the gang boxes.

6. Run remote-control wire to proper relay location in gang box.

7. Precautionary step. Relays may be burned out during plastering operations if the wires for the switches are shorted. To prevent this damage, relays should not be mounted until after plastering has been completed. If connections are made for testing pur-

poses, they should be disconnected before the plastering operation.

## FINISH WIRING

1. Connect switches and attach wall plates.

2. Make low-voltage connections to the relays, then insert the barrels of the relays through the knockouts previously removed from outlet boxes. Spring clips on the sides of the barrels will hold the relays in place.

3. Make 115-volt connections.

## USING REMOTE-CONTROL SYSTEM WHEN REMODELING

CONTROL WIRING: Small, flat, low-voltage wiring can be run behind moldings, along baseboards, or even on the surface. It is inconspicuous when properly installed. Such wiring can be fished through spaces which would not permit the use of armored or non-metallic cables. In plaster walls, the wiring can be placed in a shallow groove and plastered over.

SWITCHES: Standard switches can be replaced by one, two or three remote-control switches and mounted to the switch box by means of the mounting strap furnished with the remote-control wall plate, or a master selector switch can be used for as many as nine separate circuits.

# REMOTE CONTROL SYSTEMS

The use of surface-mounted switches makes a remote-control system practical for rewiring, because it can be mounted almost anywhere -- on door frames, brick-filled walls, very shallow partitions and similar locations, where there is no space for outlet or switch boxes.

RELAYS: Wherever possible, relays should be inserted in the outlet boxes to be controlled, in the same manner as described for new construction. Where old boxes will not accommodate relays, new boxes should be substituted or added.

MULTIPOINT SWITCHING: Where a single switch is to be replaced by multipoint switching, remove the single-pole switch and use a relay in its place. The low-voltage wire from the new switch locations are connected to the relay after a knockout has been removed. This relay is inserted in this knockout and the 115-volt leads are connected to the wires formerly connected to the switch. Use a blank cover to close the box.

## CHECKING THE INSTALLATION

Every new wiring installation, and this includes remote-control wiring, should be checked as soon as the power is turned on. In checking the system, each circuit should be tried from each switch point including the master selector switch, to see that everything is operating correctly.

# Signal, Communication Systems

A signal system in the home serves a number of useful purposes. Front and back entrance doorways are usually provided with push buttons that ring buzzers, bells, or chimes. Signals for the two entrances should be different in character of tone.

In apartment buildings, provisions are often made to release the front-door latch from the apartments. Annunciators (signal systems that register locations from which calls were made) and communication systems between rooms, are other types of equipment which may be operated as part of a signaling system.

Electric current to operate the home signal system is usually provided by using a bell-ringing transformer (on a.c.) 6 to 16-volt capacity. See Fig. H-1.

Dry cells, Fig. H-2, may also be used to operate signal systems, and are used extensively in locations where regular 115-volt current is not available. Each dry cell furnishes 1 1/2 volts. If 6 volts are needed, four cells connected in series, Fig. H-3, will be required.

H-1. Left. Typical door-bell transformer. Right. Door bell with principal parts identified.

## SWITCHES

Push-button switches, Fig. H-4, which are simply single-pole switches, are commonly used for control. In such a switch, pressure against the button causes a movable contact to meet the fixed contact and close the circuit.

A surface-mounted push-button is fastened directly to the wall where it is to be placed, with screws. Notching is required for recessed type push-buttons, but these are usually preferable because they fit flush with the surface.

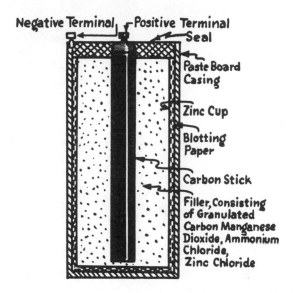

H-2.    Cutaway view of dry cell.

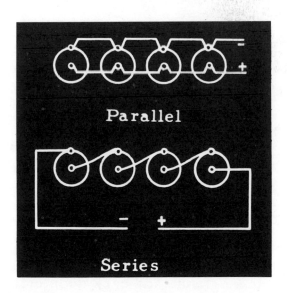

H-3.    Parallel and series dry cell hookups.

97

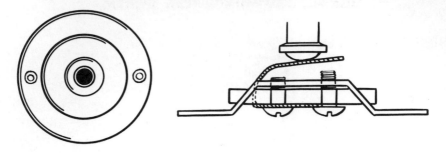

H-4.   Push-button switch. Pressure against button causes movable contact to
meet fixed contact and close circuit.

## BELLS, BUZZERS, CHIMES

Bells used in signal systems may be either the single-stroke or vibrating type. A single-stroke bell, on battery circuits, rings only once each time the button is pushed; a vibrating type bell continues to ring as long as the button is held down.

ON TRANSFORMER CIRCUITS: The single stroke bell and buzzer are recommended. They are cheaper and give no contact trouble or arcing, which is dangerous if gases accumulate.

A buzzer is similar to a bell except there is no hammer; the noise is made by the motion of the armature.

In many modern homes door chimes are used instead of bells and buzzers. Chimes are available in many designs and tones, at various prices. Most chimes are so constructed that they give different sounds when the front and back door button switches are operated. In this way persons in the home can determine from which door the chime is being operated.

SIGNAL SYSTEM INSTALLATION

Fig. H-5 shows a wiring diagram for a simple transformer-operated system. No. 14 insulated wires, one white and one black, are used to connect the transformer to the 115-volt power line. No. 18 bell wire is

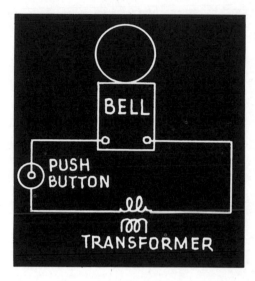

H-5.    Wiring diagram of simple transformer-operated signal system.

ordinarily used for making the chime or bell hookup. Bell wiring must be kept at least two inches away from 115-volt circuits, to comply with the Code.

Fig. H-6 shows a front and back entrance, bell-buzzer hookup. Fig. H-7 shows a wiring hookup for controlling a single bell from two or more places; Fig. H-8, how three bells may be controlled by one button, Fig. H-9 illustrates a hookup for a three-wire return signal system.

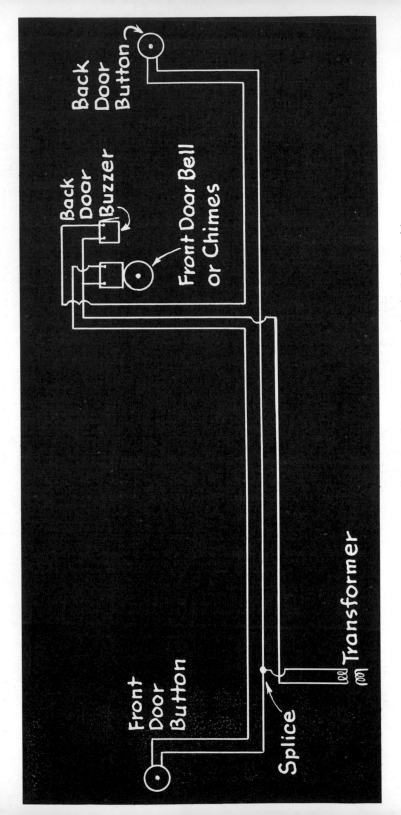

H-6.   Wiring diagram of front and back entrances, using both bell and buzzer.

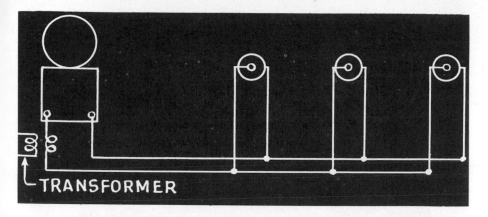

H-7.  Diagram showing how one bell may be controlled from three places.

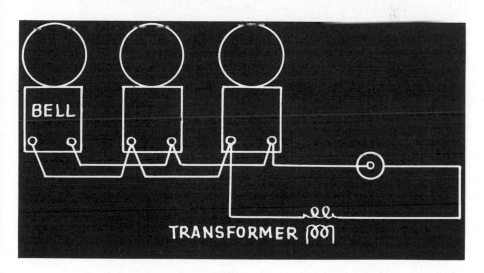

H-8.  Three bells controlled by one push-button switch.

In a new house the signal system is generally in-stalled when the house is at the lath stage -- when framing and partitions are in place and the carpenters are about ready to start lathing.

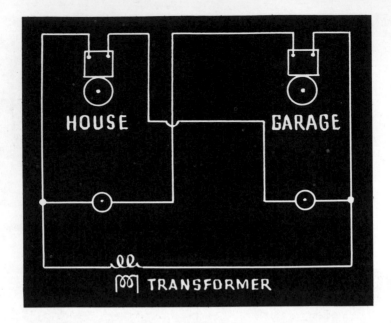

H-9.   Hookup for three-wire return signal system.

Insulated staples should be used to fasten the bell wiring to the surface. Unless prohibited by local ordinance, both wires may be placed under staples.

DOOR OPENER

Fig. H-10 shows a combination bell and door-opener circuit. In the door opener a spring forces the door bolt into place to lock the door. When the push button is pressed an electro-magnet withdraws the bolt allowing the door to be opened.

ANNUNCIATOR

The wiring diagram, Fig. H-11, shows the hookup for an annunciator using a single bell and provision for making known the location of calls from three locations.

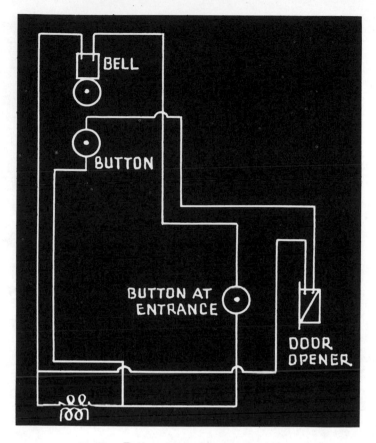

H-10.  Bell and door-opener circuit.

The annunciator indicates the location of the call until it is reset either electrically or manually. Many types of annunciators are available.

## INTER-ROOM COMMUNICATION SYSTEMS

Two general types of telephones are available for use as inter-room communications systems, flush and surface types. Flush type instruments are generally installed in new construction and surface type instruments in after-construction installations.

103

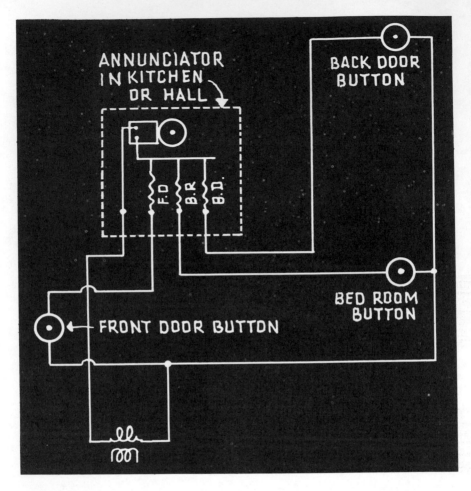

H-11.  Annunciator call system with three stations.

## TELEPHONES

Facilities for concealing telephone wiring should not be overlooked when planning a home. Outlet boxes and wiring channels are easily built into the walls during construction and make possible telephone installations of greatly improved appearance.

Modern construction practices frequently make it

impractical to fish or otherwise conceal wires after the building is completed. If wiring channels have not been provided, the cheaper alternative is to employ surface wiring which, in view of present trends toward smaller molding and baseboards and flush-type window and door frames, detracts materially from the general appearance of a finished room.

OUTLET LOCATIONS: When planning telephone outlets for a new home, it is desirable to consider the future as well as the present telephone needs of the

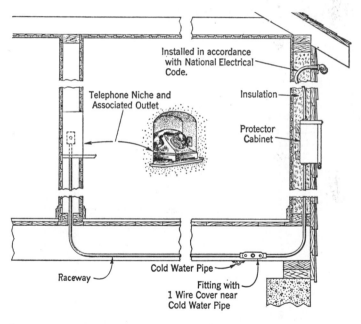

Installed in accordance with National Electrical Code.

Telephone Niche and Associated Outlet

Insulation

Protector Cabinet

Cold Water Pipe

Raceway

Fitting with 1 Wire Cover near Cold Water Pipe

H-12. Providing raceway for telephones, frame construction.

household, and the provision of additional outlets not needed initially will later be recognized as good planning and forward thinking.

In a one-story house or the first floor of a two-story house, the preferred locations for telephone outlets are:

1. A central location convenient to kitchen, dining room and living room.

2. In kitchen (where practical, such as at a planning desk location).

3. Master bedroom - of a one-story house - den, study or living room.

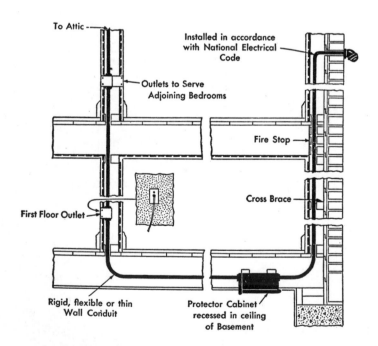

H-13. Raceway provision for telephones, brick veneer construction.

## SIGNAL, COMMUNICATION SYSTEMS

In a two-story house, one or more outlets should always be provided on the second floor to care for present and future needs. The preferred locations for these outlets are:

Master bedroom
Large hall
Guest room
Sewing room or other frequented space

Where a basement has a recreation room or other finished spaces, telephone outlets to serve such locations are desirable.

In smaller homes, a recess or niche in a wall may well serve as a telephone location. Fig. H-12 illustrates how such a recess may serve, and the necessary raceway connections for providing telephone service.

The added convenience of using portable telephones at a number of locations may be desirable in some homes. The outlet box and wiring channel arrangements are the same as for other telephones although a few more outlets may be needed.

SERVICE CONNECTIONS: A complete wiring channel installation placed during construction should include a service entrance line, as shown in Figs. H-12 and H-13, or an underground arrangement for placing the service entrance wires from the nearest telephone terminal pole or manhole to the protector cabinet. Service entrance arrangements should be discussed with the local telephone company.

INTERIOR RACEWAYS: The interior wiring channels should extend from the protector cabinet to suitable locations for the telephone sets and terminate in outlet boxes in the wall, as shown in Fig. H-13; or in certain localities, a niche or recess with an associated outlet, as shown in Fig. H-12, may be preferred.

When placing an outlet box in an interior wall common to two rooms, one wiring channel can frequently be made to serve both rooms by fastening two boxes together, as shown in Fig. H-13. Likewise, the

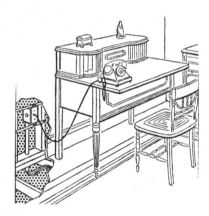

H-14.    Raceway for telephone to unfinished basement.

same channel run that serves the first floor can often be extended to the second floor, thus reducing the amount of raceway needed.

Adequate raceways may be provided by running a few feet of conduit or tubing to an unfinished part of the basement, Fig. H-14, or accessible part of the attic.

The material used for raceways will vary in different localities, depending on city building codes and regulations, as well as on the type of material most readily available.

TECHNICAL ASSISTANCE: In connection with provision for telephones, most local telephone companies maintain a service to aid anyone building or remodeling a home. Such information may be obtained by calling at the nearest telephone business office.

## RADIO-TELEVISION

It is recommended that raceway enclosures with outlet or outlets be provided to allow for convenient means of replacing antenna leads.

At the desired locations for radio and television receivers, provide outlets. From the outlets extend 3/4 inch inside diameter, non-metallic raceway to the unfinished portion of attic and also to the unfinished portion of basement (if any). In addition to the radio-television receptacles in the outlet boxes, provision should also be made for a convenient receptacle connected to a 115-volt circuit.

Since the best viewing of television requires a degree of darkness, the outlets should be placed to permit locating television receiver so that the light entering through windows will not be reflected on the picture screen.

Be sure not to install a television set under a thermostat, as it will upset the regulation during the heating season.

# Modernizing Electrical Systems

## PROBLEMS INVOLVED

Modernizing of residential electrical wiring systems involves getting cables and wires from one point to another with the least effort and minimum damaging of structural members and finished walls.

Old work frequently requires much more material than new work because it is necessary to lead the cable through channels that are readily accessible, rather than tear up ceilings, floors, walls, etc.

Solving the problems that arise requires some ingenuity on the part of the electrician or "handy man" handling the job.

## INSTALLING WALL SWITCH

To get right into the subject of modernizing old wiring we will discuss first, how to install a wall switch for a ceiling light that previously has been controlled by a pull-switch cord hanging from the light.

If the attic is open and wires to the ceiling fixture are readily accessible, the job is greatly simplified.

111

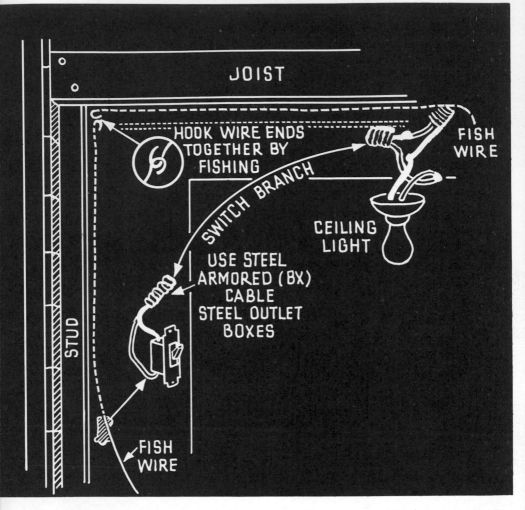

J-1.    Installing wall switch for ceiling light previously controlled by pull-
switch cord hanging from light.

An armored cable can probably be run from the ceiling outlet box to the partition plate of the wall where the switch box is to be located. A hole is drilled through this plate, and the cable run through the hole down through the wall cavity to an opening cut in the wall to take a switch box. See Fig. J-1.

112

## CUTTING OPENING IN WALL

The opening in the wall to take the switch box must be made just the right size and neatly.

First make sure there is no stud (vertical 2 x 4 to which lath, etc., is fastened) in the way. One of the best ways to determine this, is to see where the base-

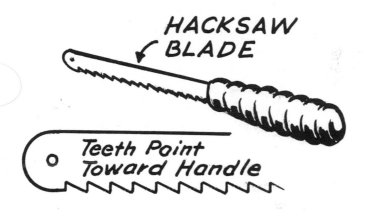

*HACKSAW BLADE*

*Teeth Point Toward Handle*

J-2.    Hacksaw blade wrapped with tape makes efficient tool for cutting openings in plastered wall.

board is nailed. Centers of wall studs are usually 16 inches apart.

Assuming that the location of the opening has been determined, the next step is to hold the switch box to be installed up to the wall and mark around it lightly, using a lead pencil. Make the opening about 1/4 inch larger each way than the box.

If the wall is wood lath and plaster, it is advisable to spot the opening so that only one lath will be cut through completely. This helps prevent cracked plaster. You can determine the location of the lath by making exploratory holes with a small drill.

An inexpensive but efficient saw for cutting wall openings may be made by wrapping one end of a hacksaw blade with friction tape, Fig. J-2. Be sure to put the tape on the proper end of the blade. Sawing is done when the saw is pulled toward you, which is opposite to the usual sawing procedure. While sawing, hold left hand against wall to help prevent cracking the plaster.

Drill a hole near one corner of the piece to be cut out, large enough to take the saw blade. While sawing, hold one hand against the plaster, to prevent pulling the plaster off the wall. Take your time and do a good, neat job.

## MOUNTING SWITCH BOX

Mounting a switch box in a wall opening, in both lath and plaster, and wallboard, is shown in Fig. J-3. The mounting ears on ends of switch boxes are adjustable to compensate for materials of various thicknesses. In making a box installation the ears should be adjusted so the front edge of the box is flush with the wall surface.

Installing armored cable is a two-man job. One man is needed to pull the cable, the other to feed it into the wall opening.

Connecting the cable to the box is easy, if the cable

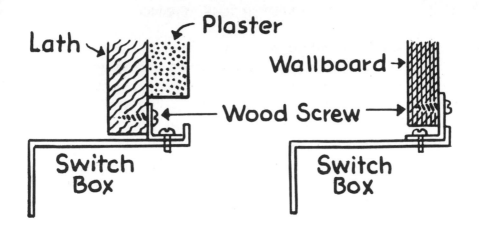

J-3.    Mounting switch box in wall opening of lath and plaster;  also wallboard.

runs into the bottom of the box. The connection is made before the box is permanently fastened in place.

If this is not practical and the connection must be made through a knockout in the end of the box, Fig. J-4, a different procedure is required; otherwise a hole for the box excessive in size will be needed. Make the wall opening large enough to take the box, plus the thickness of the wires inside the cable. Attach the connector, run the wires through the knockout opening and grasp the ends. Then, push the box into the wall opening, pull on the wires to bring the cable connector into position. Place the locknut over the connector and tighten.

## INSTALLING ADDITIONAL OUTLETS

When installing convenience outlets be sure to make a careful study of the present wiring so that the new outlets may be installed with a minimum of time and expense.

On inside partitions, it is frequently possible to run a cable from an existing outlet on one side of a wall through a groove made in the plaster between two lath back of the baseboard to the outlet on the other side of the wall. See Fig. J-5. Do not overlook this possibility.

In one-story houses, or on the second floor of two-story houses, cable can generally be run through the attic, following the procedure previously described for installing a wall switch.

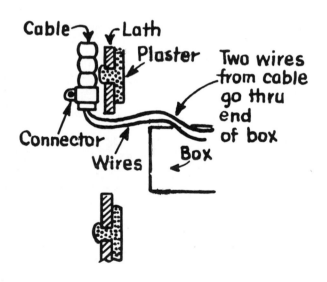

J-4.     Connecting cable to end of switch box.

On a two-story house, the procedure shown in Fig. J-6, can frequently be used to good advantage. Two pieces of heavy wire or regular electrician's "fish" lines or wires, can be used to pull the cable through the wall cavities.

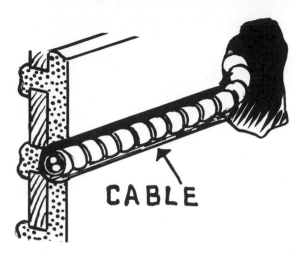

CABLE

J-5.    Running cable in groove made in plaster between lath, back of baseboard.

J-6.    Running wire from ceiling of first-floor room in two-story residence, to opening in wall provided for outlet box.

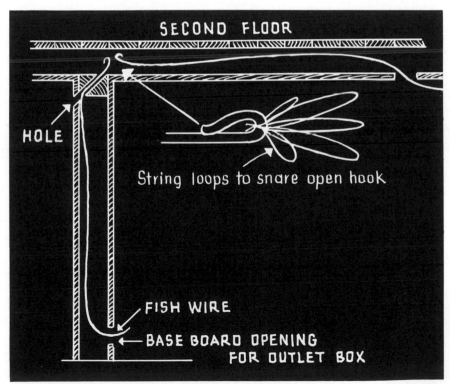

SECOND FLOOR

HOLE

String loops to snare open hook

FISH WIRE

BASE BOARD OPENING
FOR OUTLET BOX

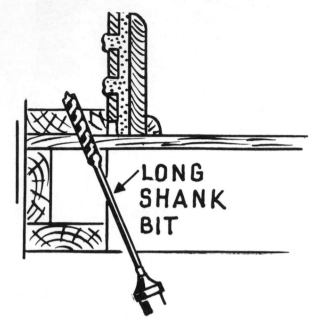

J-7.    Using long-shank bit to bore hole for cable.

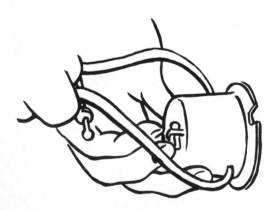

J-8.    Using caliper to measure floor outlet receptacle to determine size
hole needed.

On some wiring jobs the cable may be run from an outlet box in the basement to a spot directly under the desired location of the new outlet and an opening made through the structural member using a long-shank electrician's bit, Fig. J-7.

## FLOOR OUTLETS

Another way to provide extra outlets is to install them in the floor, Fig. J-9. In one-story homes and on the first floor of two-story homes, outlet receptacles

J-9.    Using wood screws to fasten electrical outlet in place in floor opening.

can usually be installed in the floor without cutting plaster or fishing wires through the walls. In making floor installations only floor boxes especially approved for the purpose should be used.

Floor outlets should always be installed out of traffic areas. Locations chosen for floor outlets should be far enough away from floor joists (about two inches) to provide clearance for the receptacles. Locations of floor joists may be determined by drilling a very small hole through the floor and running a wire through the hole so the measurement can be checked from underneath the floor.

Measure the floor outlet receptacle, Fig. J-8, and use an expansion bit to make a hole of the proper size to take the receptacle.

## REMOVING FLOOR BOARDS

Lifting of floor boards should be avoided wherever possible. In cases where existing structural members prevent making installations and lifting of one or more boards is necessary, special care should be used so the job can be done with minimum damage to the floor.

The first step in removing a floor board is to chisel off the tongues which hold the board in place so a portion of a board may be removed. A putty knife with the blade ground off short and sharpened to a chisel edge makes a good tool for this purpose.

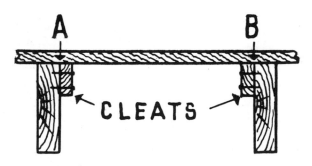

J-10.    Removing tongue-and-groove flooring board.

The tongues should be cut off the full distance between two floor joists. Location of the joists can be determined as the cutting with the chisel progresses.

Bore small holes at points A and B, Fig. J-10, then

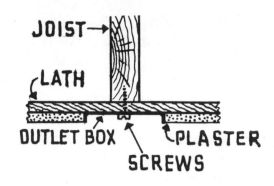

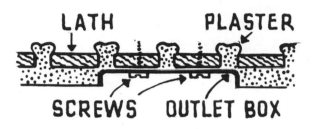

J-11.    Mounting shallow outlet boxes in old work.

use a keyhole saw to saw through the board. The flooring board which has been loosened may then be lifted and the electrical work completed. Cleats should be fastened securely to the joists to support the ends of the board, before replacing it. The holes may be filled with wood putty, or with wood plugs; plugs are usually preferable.

REPAIRING WALLPAPER

On an electrical modernizing job it is frequently necessary to make a hole in a wall that is covered with wallpaper. Removing a section of paper and replacing it is not difficult. Use a razor blade to cut the paper at the sides and bottom of the opening. Do not cut the paper at the top. Next, use a clean sponge or rag saturated with warm water to soak the portion of the paper which has been cut. After the paste has softened, lift the paper carefully, fold it upward and use a thumbtack to hold it up out of the way.

Upon completion of the wiring job, the hole in the plaster can be patched using patching plaster or plaster-of-paris, and the paper put back in place using fresh wallpaper paste.

OUTLET BOX MOUNTING

The Code specifies outlet boxes with a minimum depth of 1 1/2 inches for new work, but boxes 1/2 inch

J-12.    Using old-work bar hanger to install shallow box in ceiling. The hanger is turned so the bar lies across the lath to distribute the weight.

deep may be used on old work. Such boxes may be mounted on lath or attached to a joist or stud, as shown in Fig. J-11.

On ceiling jobs, using a bar hanger, as shown in Fig. J-12, is desirable; otherwise the weight of the fixture may damage the ceiling. Completing the installation of the ceiling fixture is shown in Fig. J-13.

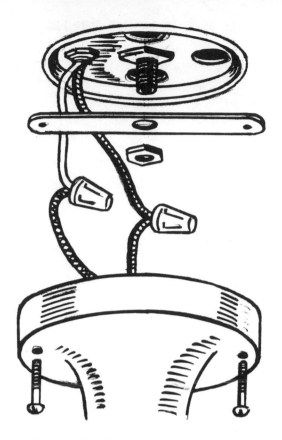

J-13.  Installing ceiling fixture.  Box used is of the shallow type.

## PLUG-IN MOLDING

Plug-in molding -- steel channel or raceway installed above the baseboard or at chair-rail height to carry electrical wiring, may be used not only in modernizing electrical systems, but also for new construction as well.

The type of plug-in molding which will be discussed in this section is called Plugmold and is made

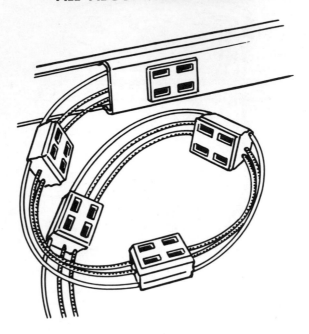

J-14.  Plug-in molding for use above baseboard, with factory-wired receptacles (Plugmold 2000).

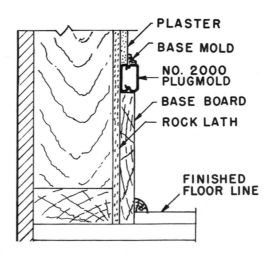

PLASTER

BASE MOLD

NO. 2000
PLUGMOLD

BASE BOARD

ROCK LATH

FINISHED
FLOOR LINE

J-15.  Plugmold installed above baseboard, semi-flush with plaster. Plugmold may be surface mounted where wall back of baseboard is same thickness as above baseboard, above kitchen cabinets and home workshop benches, etc.

by the Wiremold Company. See Figs. J-14, J-15, J-16 and J-17.

In using Plugmold 2000, these steps are necessary to complete an installation:

1. Mount the required lengths of base in continuous runs. The base is fastened to the studs using

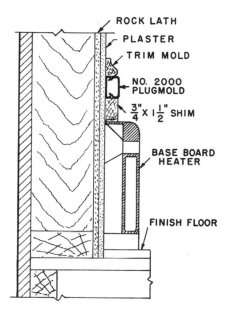

J-16.    Plugmold being used above baseboard heater panels.

wood screws. Screw holes in base are provided by removing screw knockouts. Start the job by installing corner elbows.

2. Snap factory pre-wired receptacles into raceway cover. The raceway cover and the pre-wired receptacles come in five foot lengths and provide

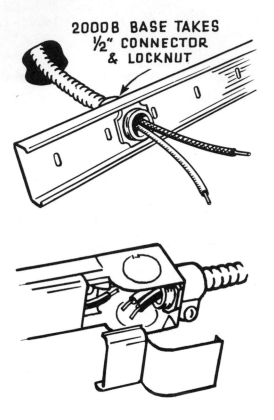

**2000B BASE TAKES ½" CONNECTOR & LOCKNUT**

J-17.   Connecting feeder line to Plugmold base.

outlets every 30 inches. Both the cover and the pre-wired receptacles are also available in three and six-foot lengths with receptacles either six or eighteen inches on centers.

3. Snap raceway cover with receptacles inserted into the base. Attach fittings with snap-over covers. Raceway cover may be easily pried off base using a screwdriver.

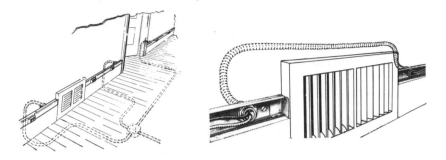

J-18.    Bypassing obstructions in Plugmold wiring.

Connecting feeder lines to the Plugmold base and bypassing obstructions are shown in Figs. J-17 and J-18. Fig. J-19 shows Plugmold being used along the backboard of a workbench in a home workshop.

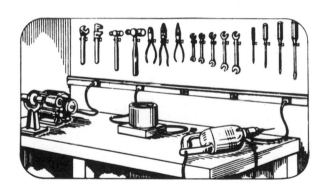

J-19.    Plugmold in sections with closely spaced outlets being used along back-board of bench in home workshop.

# *Outlet Requirements by Rooms*

In this section are presented the requirements of an adequate wiring system for a modern dwelling, as recommended by the Industry Committee on Interior Wiring Design and other nationally recognized authorities. The application of these recommendations to wiring jobs will result in efficient and effective electrical installation.

## ELECTRICAL SYMBOLS

Electrical symbols, Fig. K-1, are the electrician's system of "shorthand". They provide a simplified way of showing on blueprints and building plans, what electrical service is to be provided, where outlets and switches are to be installed, etc. See also Fig. K-2.

### K-1 General Outlets

Ceiling Wall

Ⓞ —Ⓞ Outlet.

Ⓑ —Ⓑ Blanked Outlet.

Ⓓ Drop Cord.

Ⓔ —Ⓔ Electrical Outlet; for use only when circle used alone might be confused with columns, plumbing symbols, etc.

Ⓕ —Ⓕ Fan Outlet.

Ⓙ —Ⓙ Junction Box.

Ⓛ —Ⓛ Lampholder.

Ⓛ PS —Ⓛ PS Lampholder with Pull Switch.

Ⓢ —Ⓢ Pull Switch.

Ⓒ —Ⓒ Clock Outlet. (Specify Voltage)

# ALL ABOUT HOUSE WIRING

K-1.   Electrical symbols.

## CONVENIENCE OUTLETS

Duplex Convenience Outlet.

Convenience Outlet other than Duplex. 1 = Single, 3 = Triplex, etc.

Weatherproof Convenience Outlet. (WP)

Range Outlet. (R)

Switch and Convenience Outlet. (S)

Radio and Convenience Outlet. (R)

Special Purpose Outlet. (Des. in Spec.)

Floor Outlet.

## SWITCH OUTLETS

$S$   Single Pole Switch.

$S_2$   Double Pole Switch.

$S_3$   Three Way Switch.

$S_4$   Four Way Switch.

$S_D$   Automatic Door Switch.

$S_E$   Electrolier Switch.

$S_K$   Key Operated Switch.

$S_P$   Switch and Pilot Lamp.

$S_{CB}$   Circuit Breaker.

$S_{WCB}$   Weatherproof Circuit Breaker.

$S_{MC}$   Momentary Contact Switch.

$S_{RC}$   Remote Control Switch.

$S_{WP}$   Weatherproof Switch.

## SPECIAL OUTLETS

$O_{a, b, c, etc.}$

$_{a, b, c, etc.}$

$S_{a, b, c, etc.}$

Any Standard Symbol as given here with the addition of a lower case subscript letter may be used to designate some special variation of Standard Equipment of particular interest in a specific set of Architectural Plans.

When used they must be listed in the Key of Symbols on each drawing and if necessary further described in the specifications.

## SPECIAL AUXILIARY OUTLETS

$\square_{a, b, c, etc.}$

Subscript letters refer to notes on plans or detailed description in specifications.

Push Button.

Buzzer.

Bell.

Annunciator.

Outside Telephone.

Interconnecting Telephone.

Bell Ringing Transformer (T)

Electric Door Opener. (D)

Maid's Signal Plug. (M)

Radio Outlet. (R)

Interconnection Box.

Battery.

—·—·— Auxiliary System Circuits.

Note: Any line without further designation indicates a 2-wire system. For a greater number of wires designate in manner similar to — 12 No. 18W-¾" C. — or designate by number corresponding to listing in Schedule.

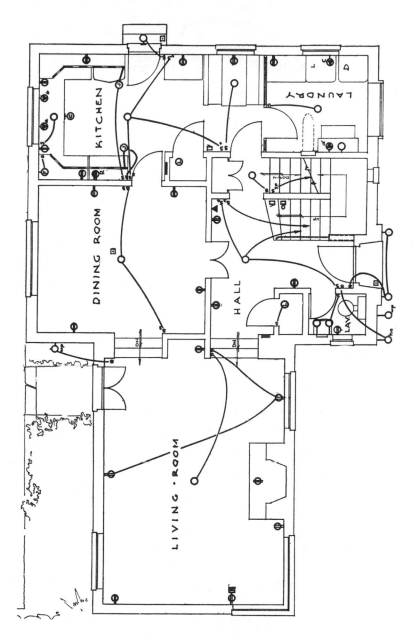

K-2.    Floor plan showing use of electrical symbols.

K-3.    The term Lighting Outlet is meant to imply the box in which the conductors are terminated and to which various types of lighting fixtures may be fastened.

## LIVING ROOM

### (Also Library, Den and Sunroom)

## LIGHTING OUTLETS

One ceiling outlet, wall switch controlled, should be provided. Refer to Figs. K-3 and K-4. Rooms of a length more than twice the width should have two ceiling outlets. The ceiling outlets may be omitted provided wall, cove or valance lighting outlets, wall switch controlled are substituted.

Balanced illumination in a room is the ultimate purpose of lighting. Fixed lighting equipment forms an essential part of provisions for balanced illumination.

Although often omitted in former years, recent developments in fixtures and fluorescent lighting indicate a return to previous practices. This makes it

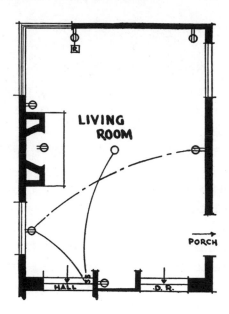

K-4.  Living room layout showing location of both lighting and convenience outlets.

advisable to provide outlets (ceiling, wall cove, valance, etc.) with proper switch controls, even though installation of fixtures is not immediately contemplated, especially with television receivers now in vogue.

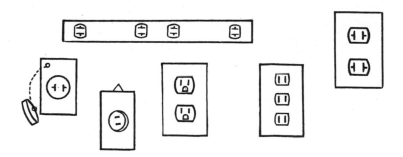

K-5.  Convenience outlets are available in many different forms.  The term Convenience Outlet is meant to imply the plug-in receptacle, as well as the box in which it is housed.

## CONVENIENCE OUTLETS

Convenience outlets, Fig. K-5, should be placed so that no point along the floor line in any usable wall space, unbroken by a doorway, is more than six feet from an outlet in that space (two or more outlets to be wall switch controlled). Wall spaces less than three feet in length at the floor are not considered usable. Install one convenience outlet flush in mantel shelf, where construction permits.

It is recommended that at one of the switch locations a convenience outlet be provided for the use of a vacuum cleaner and other portable appliances. Outlets for the use of clocks, radios, television, decorative lighting, etc., in bookcases and other suitable locations are recommended.

## SPECIAL WIRING

Special wiring should be provided for a heating system thermostat, door chimes and should be considered for a room cooler, also humidifiers, and a timer for automatic light control (turns light on and off at pre-determined times).

## DINING ROOMS

(Also Dinette and Breakfast Room)

## LIGHTING OUTLETS

One ceiling outlet, multiple wall switch controlled,

Fig. K-6. Additional outlets may be desired for decorative or subdued type of lighting. Cove and valance lighting are of this type. Any such additional outlets installed should be switch controlled at convenient locations.

## CONVENIENCE OUTLETS

Convenience outlets should be placed so that no point along the floor line in any usable wall space

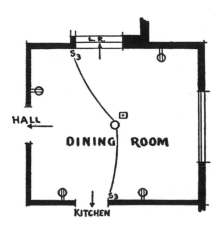

K-6.　Dining room outlet requirements.

unbroken by a doorway is more than 10 feet from an outlet in that space. Wall spaces less than three feet in length at the floor line are not considered usable. In dinettes, breakfast rooms, or other small dining areas, one of these outlets to be adjacent to the table and slightly above table height.

## KITCHEN

### (Also Kitchenette and Pantry)

LIGHTING OUTLETS

One ceiling outlet for general illumination, multiple wall switch controlled, Fig. K-7, also, one ceiling or wall outlet at sink, switch controlled.

Additional local illumination at work areas for food preparation, cooking, serving, etc., is recommended. It

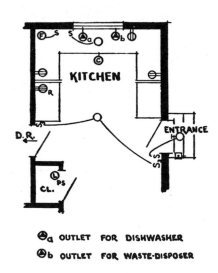

K-7.  Outlet requirements for kitchen.

is suggested that outlets be considered for inside lighting of large cabinets.

## CONVENIENCE OUTLETS

One outlet for every four feet frontage of kitchen work surface; outlets located for greatest convenience. By kitchen work surface is meant all of the work area, approximately 36 inches above the floor, exclusive of the cooking range surface and the sink surface.

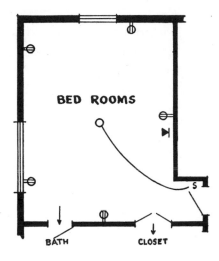

K-8.   Bedroom wiring layout, showing suggested locations for both lighting and convenience outlets.

If areas are to be divided by space, at least one outlet should be provided at each such area. An outlet should also be provided at the refrigerator location. All outlets with the exception of the one provided for the refrigerator, should be located approximately 44 inches above the floor line.

An additional outlet is desirable for space in the

kitchen which might be used for ironing purposes. Such an outlet should be located about 48 inches above the finished floor line.

## SPECIAL PURPOSE OUTLETS

One outlet for each of the following pieces of equipment: Range, clock (recessed receptable high on wall, and in location easily visible from all parts of the kitchen), kitchen ventilating fan, dishwasher, towel drying cabinet, chimes or bell-buzzer system, garbage disposer, home freezer, appliance timer, intercommunication set, also outside telephone.

## LAUNDRY - UTILITY

### LIGHTING OUTLETS

Lighting outlets should be provided for: Ceiling light; lights over washer, ironer, dryer, furnace, workbench.

Provide wall switch control for ceiling lights; remaining outlets may be equipped with pull-chain controlled fixtures.

### CONVENIENCE OUTLETS

One outlet for each of following: Washer, portable fan, hotplate for starch, ironer, hand iron, radio, sewing machine, floor polisher.

SPECIAL PURPOSE OUTLETS

Special outlets in laundry - utility for: Clothes dryer, air conditioning system, electrostatic air cleaner, home freezer, built-in ventilating fan, water heater, intercommunication set.


BEDROOMS

LIGHTING OUTLETS

One ceiling outlet, wall switch controlled. See Fig. K-8. Additional outlets for decorative lighting and illumination at mirrors is suggested. Master switch control, in the master bedroom, for selected interior and exterior lights is suggested for consideration.

CONVENIENCE OUTLETS

Convenience outlets should be placed so that no point along the floor line in any usable wall space, unbroken by a doorway, is more than six feet from an outlet in that space. Wall spaces less than three feet in length at the floor line are not considered usable.

SPECIAL PURPOSE OUTLETS

The installation of one heavy-duty special purpose outlet in each bedroom for the connection of a portable space heater, is recommended, particularly for warmer climates in which a small amount of local heat is sufficient. Such outlets may also be used for operating individual air cooling equipment during hot weather. Also to be considered, should be providing outlets for thermostat (furnace control) and intercommunication set, likewise, outside telephone.

## BATHROOM

### (Also Lavatories)

### LIGHTING OUTLETS

One outlet at each side of the mirror, wall switch controlled. One ceiling outlet in completely enclosed

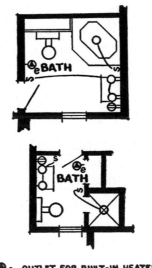

**⊕e OUTLET FOR BUILT-IN HEATER**

K-9.  Bathroom wiring layout.

shower compartment, controlled by a switch outside the compartment. Bathrooms having an area of 60 square feet or more should be equipped with a wall switch controlled ceiling outlet. Refer to Fig. K-9.

## CONVENIENCE OUTLETS

One convenience outlet near mirror and at a height of three to four feet above the floor line.

The provision of outlets for the connection of various health devices, such as sun lamps is recommended. It is recommended too that a switch controlled night light be installed.

## SPECIAL PURPOSE OUTLETS

It is recommended that each bathroom be equipped with an outlet for the connection of a built-in wall type space heater.

## RECREATION ROOM

## LIGHTING OUTLETS

One ceiling outlet, wall switch controlled, for each 150 square feet of floor area; if recreation room is fitted with snack bar, provision should be made for installing recessed fixture over bar. Ceiling outlets, except over snack bar, may be omitted provided, wall, cove or valance lighting outlets, wall switch controlled, are substituted. Note Fig. K-10.

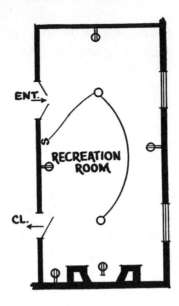

K-10.    Recreation room wiring layout.

## CONVENIENCE OUTLETS

Convenience outlets placed so that no point along floor line in any usable wall space, unbroken by doorway, is more than 10 feet from an outlet in that space. Wall spaces less than three feet in length at the floor line are not considered usable. Install one convenience outlet flush in mantel shelf, where construction permits.

It is recommended that at one of the switch locations a receptacle outlet be provided for the use of vacuum cleaners and other portable appliances. Outlets for the use of clocks, radios, television, phonographs, motion picture projector, decorative lighting, air conditioner, odor bans, etc., in bookcases and other suitable locations are recommended.

# OUTLET REQUIREMENTS BY ROOMS

## BASEMENT UTILITY SPACE

### LIGHTING OUTLETS

One lighting outlet for each enclosed space, and one for furnace location, each pull-chain controlled. Sufficient additional outlets to provide at least one for each 150 square feet of open space, pull-chain or switch controlled.

A light at the head and foot of basement stairway (multiple switch controlled) is provided by requirements of section of Code on Stairways. Wall switches, near doors, for lights in enclosed spaces, or door type switches, are recommended in place of pull-chain control.

### CONVENIENCE OUTLETS

Outlet at furnace to serve cleaning and maintenance tools used in connection with heating plant.

### SPECIAL PURPOSE OUTLETS

One for electrical equipment used in connection with furnace operation. Installation of an outlet, multiple-switch controlled from desirable locations throughout the house, is recommended for the connection of a summer cooling fan. Such a fan may, as an alternate, be installed in the attic.

In cases where the laundry is in the basement instead of utility room, outlets should be installed as discussed in the Laundry-Utility section.

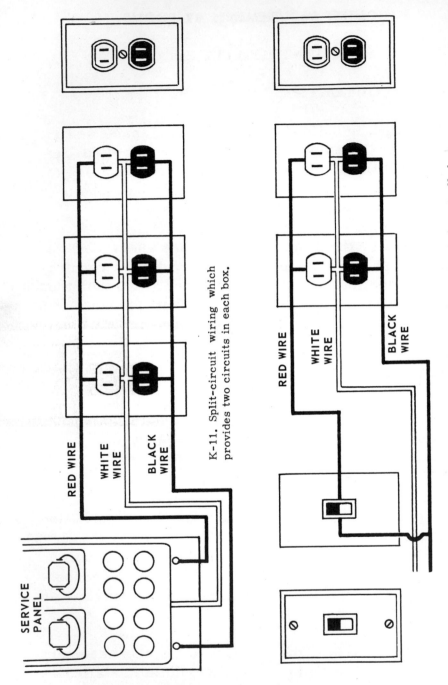

K-11. Split-circuit wiring which provides two circuits in each box.

K-11A. Split-circuit wiring with upper half switch controlled.

RED WIRE

WHITE WIRE

BLACK WIRE

RED WIRE

WHITE WIRE

BLACK WIRE

SERVICE PANEL

## SPLIT-CIRCUIT WIRING

Fig. K-11, shows a split-circuit wiring arrangement where two separate circuits operate in each box. Such wiring is especially desirable where there is a need to balance a load of heavy appliances in the kitchen, or in the home workshop.

Three No. 12 wires (red, white and black) are required. These run from the main switch box, as indicated in the drawing. The white or neutral wire, should be connected to the silver-colored terminals of both the upper and lower receptacles. Connect the red wire to the brass-colored terminals of the upper receptacles, and the black wire to the brass-colored terminals of the lower receptacles. This provides two circuits for each box. Each circuit is independent of the other.

The wiring diagram, Fig. K-11A, shows split-circuit wiring similar to the wiring shown in Fig. K-11, except one circuit (upper) is switch controlled. This arrangement is commonly used for living and bedrooms.

## RECEPTION HALL

One ceiling lighting outlet, wall switch controlled. The ceiling outlet may be omitted provided wall, cove or valance lighting outlets, wall switch controlled, are substituted.

Convenience outlets placed so that no point along the floor line in any usable wall space, unbroken by a doorway, is more than 10 feet from an outlet in that space.

## OTHER HALLS

One lighting outlet for each 15 linear feet of hall-way, multiple wall switch controlled. A hall of irregular shape may require closer spacing. A switch controlled night light is recommended for halls serving bed-rooms. One convenience outlet for each 15 linear feet of hall, measured along center line. It is recommended that at one of the switch locations a receptacle outlet be provided for the connection of vacuum cleaners and other portable appliances.

## STAIRWAYS

One lighting outlet on each floor, one to illuminate head, and the other the foot of stairway; a separate multiple switch at the head and foot of stairway.

The above provisions do not apply to stairways giving access to attics used for storage purposes only. Additional lighting outlets are recommended for large landing areas. Switches should (whenever possible) be grouped under one plate, and never located so close to steps that a fall might result from a misstep while reaching for the switch.

It is recommended that at one of the switch loca-tions a receptacle outlet be provided for the use of vacuum cleaners.

## CLOSETS

An outlet for lighting in every closet three feet or more deep or having a floor area of 10 square feet or more except where shelving would make any light source ineffective. See Fig. K-12.

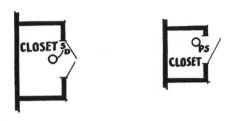

K-12.   Closet wiring layout.

Closet lighting outlets should be located at the lock side of the door and at a height sufficient (seven feet or more) to prevent the fixture being used as a clothes hook. The installation of wall switches near the closet door, or door-type switches, is recommended in place of the pull-chain control.

## EXTERIOR ENTRANCES

One ceiling outlet or one or two wall outlets as architecture dictates, wall switch controlled, Fig. K-13.

The principal lighting requirements at entrances are illumination of the steps leading to the entrance and of the faces of people at the door. Single waterproof

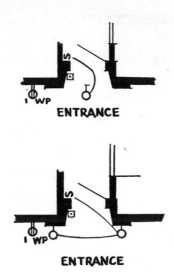

K-13.   Lighting exterior entrances.

convenience outlet at front entrance, located approximately 18 inches above grade line.

It is recommended that this outlet be controlled by a wall switch inside the door. The outlet is for outdoor decorative lighting, and for appliances that may be used outside. Additional outlets along the exterior of the house, about 18 inches above grade, located to serve decorative garden treatments, for electrical accessories such as hedge trimmers, etc., are recommended. Such outlets should be switch controlled.

### COVERED PORCHES

One lighting outlet for each 150 square feet of porch area, wall switch controlled, Fig. K-14.

Where an exterior entrance enters on a covered porch, the lighting outlets as required for the Exterior Entrance may be considered as satisfying one of the lighting outlets required for Covered Porches.

One convenience outlet for each 15 linear feet of house wall bordering porch.

## TERRACES AND PATIOS

The installation of a lighting outlet on the building wall or on a post, centrally located in the area, is recommended for providing fixed general illumination. Such outlets should be wall switch controlled just inside house door opening onto area.

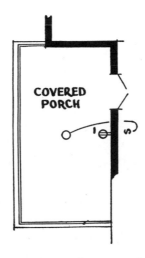

K-14.   Wiring layout for covered porch.

Waterproof convenience outlets should be located approximately 18 inches above the floor line, for each

15 linear feet of house wall bordering terrace or patio.

It may also be desirable to provide weatherproof convenience outlets located with and concealed by shrubbery for spotlighting.

## GARAGE

One interior lighting outlet, wall switch controlled, for one or two-car garage; and sufficient additional wall-switched lighting outlets to provide illumination for work to be done. If garage is detached from residence, provide one exterior outlet, multiple switch controlled from garage and residence.

Where garage is attached to the residence, an exterior lighting outlet, wall switch controlled, is recommended.

One convenience outlet for a one or two-car garage and sufficient additional outlets to provide one for each two-car storage area.

Outlets to be located approximately 48 inches above the floor. If a workbench is to be used in the garage, it is recommended that both a lighting outlet and convenience receptacle outlet be installed at the chosen location.

Some local codes call for extension cords with lamp guard and handle to be part of garage installation.

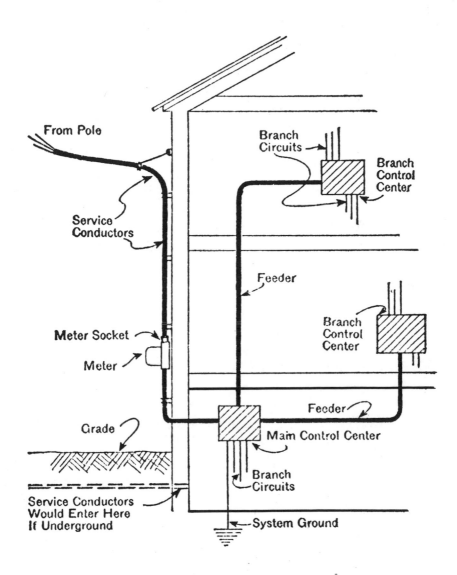

K-15. Schematic drawing of electrical distribution system showing control centers near centers of load.

## CONTROL CENTERS, FEEDERS

In the past, it has been the custom to locate all circuit protective disconnects in one location. This location frequently was in the basement or some other equally inconvenient space.

The trend in modern wiring is toward placing control-centers near "the center of load". See Fig. K-15. The kitchen, laundry and utility rooms have the greatest portion of the electrical load. For this reason, it is desirable to locate one of the control centers in such an area. This will result in the branch circuits being short in length.

In addition to greater convenience to the occupants, centrally placed control-centers mean less voltage drop and give more efficient operation of the electrical equipment, at a lower operating expense, and frequently at a lower initial cost.

In laying out a system with several control centers, every reasonable effort should be made to place the centers in readily accessible locations, at which locations the protective fuses and disconnects controlling the several branch circuits can be grouped for convenience and safety of operation.

Control center panels are available which are small in size, neat in appearance and may be flush mounted when desired.

| ELECTRIC OUTLETS | | Living Room | Den | Dining Room | Kitchen | Laundry | Bedroom 1 | Bedroom 2 | Bedroom 3 | Bath - 1 | Bath - 2 | Recreation Room | Utility Area | Halls - Stairs | Attic | Garage | Exterior | TOTALS | UNIT COST | TOTAL COST |
|---|---|---|---|---|---|---|---|---|---|---|---|---|---|---|---|---|---|---|---|---|
| | | | | | | | | | | | | | | | | | | | | |
| Ceiling | ○ | | | | | | | | | | | | | | | | | | | |
| Wall | ⊢○ | | | | | | | | | | | | | | | | | | | |
| Fan | Ⓕ | | | | | | | | | | | | | | | | | | | |
| Junction | Ⓙ | | | | | | | | | | | | | | | | | | | |
| Lampholder | Ⓛ | | | | | | | | | | | | | | | | | | | |
| Clock Rec'p. | Ⓒ | | | | | | | | | | | | | | | | | | | |
| Duplex Rec'p. | ⊖ | | | | | | | | | | | | | | | | | | | |
| Duplex Rec'p. Weatherproof | ⊖wp | | | | | | | | | | | | | | | | | | | |
| Range Rec'p. | ⊜R | | | | | | | | | | | | | | | | | | | |
| Rec'p. & Switch | ⊖s | | | | | | | | | | | | | | | | | | | |
| Rec'p. & Radio | Ⓡ⊖ | | | | | | | | | | | | | | | | | | | |
| Special Purpose | ▲ | | | | | | | | | | | | | | | | | | | |
| Floor Receptacle | ◉ | | | | | | | | | | | | | | | | | | | |
| Switch | S | | | | | | | | | | | | | | | | | | | |
| Switch - 3 Way | $S_3$ | | | | | | | | | | | | | | | | | | | |
| Switch - 4 Way | $S_4$ | | | | | | | | | | | | | | | | | | | |
| Switch - Door | $S_D$ | | | | | | | | | | | | | | | | | | | |
| Push Button | ▣ | | | | | | | | | | | | | | | | | | | |
| Chime | ⧖ | | | | | | | | | | | | | | | | | | | |
| Telephone | ▲ | | | | | | | | | | | | | | | | | | | |
| " (Intercom) | △ | | | | | | | | | | | | | | | | | | | |
| Bell Transformer | Ⓣ | | | | | | | | | | | | | | | | | | | |
| Loadcenters | ▬ | | | | | | | | | | | | | | | | | | | |
| Electric Heater | Ⓗ | | | | | | | | | | | | | | | | | | | |
| Pull Switch | PS | | | | | | | | | | | | | | | | | | | |
| | | | | | | | | | | | | | | | | | | | | |
| | | | | | | | | | | | | | | | | | | | | |
| TOTALS | | | | | | | | | | | | | | | | | | | | |

K-16.   Chart for making room-by-room check of outlets required.

## SIMPLE SPECIFICATION FORM

The following material is intended as a guide in preparing the wiring specifications for dwellings of small and medium size.

Some additional provisions may be found necessary for very large houses although these can be included merely as extra articles. Similarly, for very small houses, certain articles may be omitted.

All outlets, the locations of wall switches, and the outlet or outlets controlled by each switch should be shown clearly on the floor plans which must be considered as an essential part of the plans, or contract.

**SPECIFICATIONS FOR ELECTRIC WIRING IN THE DWELLING TO BE ERECTED AT ——————— FOR ———————**

1. GENERAL
   The installation of electric wiring and equipment shall conform with local regulations, the National Electrical Code, and the requirements of the local electric service company. All materials shall be new and shall be listed by Underwriters' Laboratories, Incorporated, as conforming to its standards, in every case where such a standard has been established for the particular type of material in question.

2. GUARANTEE
   The contractor shall leave his work in proper order and, without additional charge, replace any work or material which develops defects, except from ordinary wear and tear, within one year from the date of the final certificate of approval.

3. WIRING METHODS
   Interior wiring shall be _____. No exposed wiring shall be installed except in unfinished portions of basement, utility room, garage, attic, and other spaces that may be unfinished.

4. SERVICE ENTRANCE conductors shall be three No. ____ wires.

_____
(Fill in wiring method)

5. SERVICE-EQUIPMENT shall consist of _____
_____
_____

# OUTLET REQUIREMENTS BY ROOMS

### 6. FIFTEEN-AMPERE BRANCH CIRCUITS

At least _____ 15-ampere branch circuits shall be installed to supply all lighting outlets and all convenience outlets except those which are supplied by appliance branch circuits. The total number of outlets shall as nearly as possible be divided equally between these circuits. In each living room, library, sun room, bedroom, and each other principal room, the outlets shall be divided between two or more branch circuits.

### 7. APPLIANCE BRANCH CIRCUITS

Two appliance branch circuits shall be installed to supply all convenience outlets in the dining room, breakfast room, kitchen and pantry (except clock outlet), and laundry. These circuits shall be so installed that convenience outlets served by both circuits will be available in both the kitchen and the laundry.

### 8. BRANCH CIRCUIT EQUIPMENT shall be _____

_____

(Fill in type of equipment)

### 9. OUTLETS AND SWITCHES

Lighting outlets, convenience outlets complete with receptacles, and switches shall be installed as shown on the plans.

Unless otherwise shown on plans, the height of outlets above floor shall be approximately:

Switches. . . . . . . . . . . . . . . . . . . . . . . . . . . . . . . . . . . . . . . . . . . . . . . . . . . . . . . .48 inches

Convenience outlets. . . . . . . . . . . . . . . . . . . . . . . . . . . . . . . . . . . . . . . . . . . .18 inches

### 10. SPECIAL PURPOSE OUTLETS AND CIRCUITS shall be installed as shown on the plans. The circuits shall be:

| Circuits for | No. of Wires | Size |
|---|---|---|
| _____ | _____ | _____ |
| _____ | _____ | _____ |
| _____ | _____ | _____ |
| _____ | _____ | _____ |

# *Miscellaneous*

## APPLIANCE CAPACITIES
## ELECTRICAL CONSUMPTION

Electrical equipment used in the home may be classified according to fixed location appliances and portable appliances.

Fig. L-1, shows a list of major fixed-location appliances, and their approximate wattages; also gives information on the cost per hour to operate small appliances at four different rates.

Fig. L-2, lists a number of portable appliances and indicates the approximate wattages and estimated annual kilowatt-hour consumption.

The cost of operating any single appliance for one hour may be determined by dividing the wattage of the appliance by 1,000 as there are 1,000 watts in a kilowatt, and multiplying the result by the rate per kilowatt hour.

L-1  Major Fixed Appliances for the Home
Electrical Capacity, Consumption and Energy Expense

| FIXED APPLIANCES | CAPACITY WATTS (Approx.) | ESTIMATED ANNUAL KWH* |
|---|---|---|
| 1. Refrigerator. . . . . . . | 200 (1/6 hp) | 350 |
| 2. Range . . . . . . . . . . . | 7 to 14 kw | 1250 |
| 3. Fan (Kitchen) . . . . . . | 45 | 40 |
| 4. Clock (Kitchen) . . . . . | 2 | 17 |
| 5. Water Heater . . . . . . | 1 to 3 kw | 3400 |
| 6. Clothes Washer. . . . . | (See Note 1) | 75 |
| 7. Ironer . . . . . . . . . . . | 1650 | 140 |
| 8. Heating Plant . . . . . . (Motors & Controls) | 700 | (Varies with local conditions) |
| 9. Dishwasher. . . . . . . . | 1150 | 65 |
| 10. Bathroom Heater. . . . | 1000 to 1500 | 90 |
| 11. Food Waste Disposer. | 300 (1/4 hp) | 10 |
| 12. | | |
| 12. Clothes Dryer. . . . . . | 1500 and 4500 | 365 |
| 13. Home Freezer. . . . . . | 350 | 600 |
| 14. Air Conditioning . . . . | 3100 | (Varies with local conditions) |

*Source:  Edison Electric Institute

Note 1.
Wringer type--normal 375 watts;  with wringer in
in operation, approximately 450 watts.
Spinner type--normal 375 watts;  with spinner basket

accelerating, 800 to 1600 watts, depending on clothes load in basket.

Laundromat--normal 350 watts; during acceleration at beginning of spin cycle 800 to 1200 watts, depending on clothes load in basket.

Cost per hour to operate appliances

| Wattage consumed by Appliances | If rate is 3¢ per KWH | If rate is 4¢ per KWH | If rate is 5¢ per KWH | If rate is 6¢ per KWH |
|---|---|---|---|---|
| 100 watts | 10 hrs for only 3¢ | 7 1/2 hrs for only 3¢ | 6 hrs for only 3¢ | 5 hrs for only 3¢ |
| 300 watts | 3 hrs for only 2.7¢ | 2 1/2 hrs for only 3¢ | 2 hrs for only 3¢ | 1 2/3 hrs for only 3¢ |
| 500 watts | 2 hrs for only 3¢ | 1 hr for only 3¢ | 1 1/5 hrs for only 3¢ | 1 hr for only 3¢ |
| 700 watts | 1.4 hrs for only 3¢ | 1.1 hrs for only 3¢ | 1 hr for only 3.5¢ | 1 hr for only 4.2¢ |
| 1000 watts | 1 hr for only 3¢ | 1 hr for only 4¢ | 1 hr for only 5¢ | 1 hr for only 6¢ |

L-1.  **Major fixed appliances for the home. Electrical capacity, consumption and energy expense.**

# SYMPTOMS OF INADEQUATE WIRING

(a) Frequent tripping of circuit breakers or blowing of fuses.

| APPLIANCES | NUMBER PER FAMILY | CAPACITY WATTS* (Approx.) | ESTIMATED ANNUAL KWH* |
|---|---|---|---|
| 1. Bottle Warmer | 1 | 450 | 10 |
| 2. Clock | 3 to 5 | 2 | 17 |
| 3. Coffee Maker | 1 | Up to 1000 | 125 |
| 4. Comforter | 1 to 2 | 215 | 150 |
| 5. Cooker (Egg) | 1 | 600 | 15 |
| 6. Cooker (Fireless) | 1 | 650 | 75 |
| 7. Corn Popper | 1 | 600 | 5 |
| 8. Curling Iron | 1 | 20 | 5 |
| 9. Fan (Desk) | 1 to 3 | 75 | 20 |
| 10. Floor Polisher | 1 | 200 | 15 |
| 11. Fruit Juice Extractor | 1 | 50 | 5 |
| 12. Grill | 1 | Up to 1000 | 35 |
| 13. Hair Dryer | 1 | 100 | 5 |
| 14. Hand Iron | 1 to 2 | 1000 | 125 |
| 15. Heater (Radiant) | 1 | Up to 1000 | 100 |
| 16. Heating Pad | 1 | 60 | 3 |
| 17. Hot Plate | 1 | 1000 | 70 |
| 18. Immersion Heater | 1 | 200 | 5 |
| 19. Mixer (Drink) | 1 | 50 | 5 |
| 20. Radio | | | |
| (Standard Broadcast) | 2 to 6 | 100 | 100 |
| (Television) | 1 | 500 | 100 |
| 21. Roaster | 1 | 1650 | 300 |
| 22. Room Cooler | 2 to 3 | Up to 1000 | 1500 |
| 23. Sewing Machine | 1 | 75 | 10 |
| 24. Shaver | 1 to 2 | 10 | 2 |
| 25. Small Tool Motor | 1 | 100 | 10 |
| 26. Soldering Iron | 1 | 150 | 2 |
| 27. Sun Lamp | 1 | 400 | 25 |
| 28. Toaster | 1 | 1150 | 50 |
| 29. Vacuum Cleaner | 1 | 200 | 20 |
| 30. Vibrator | 1 | 50 | 2 |
| 31. Waffle Baker | 1 | 1000 | 15 |

*The figures in watts and kwh are based on one appliance.

L-2. Electrical portable appliances used in the home.

CAUSE: Overloaded circuits.

REMEDY: Subdivide circuits, providing individual circuits for important equipment.

(b) Dimming or blinking of lights when motors start . . . on refrigerators, food freezers, washing machines, water systems, and other motor-operated household equipment.

CAUSE: Motors on same circuits with lights.

REMEDY: Provide separate circuits of adequate size for motors.

(c) Heating appliances, including range, water heaters, etc., slow to reach temperature.

CAUSE: Circuit wires too small.

REMEDY: Replace with proper size wires.

(d) Excessive use of extension cords with multiple receptacles.

CAUSE: Not enough outlets.

REMEDY: Install outlets on planned basis.

(e) Tripping of main circuit breakers or blowing of main fuses at service location, without apparent reason.

CAUSE: Service equipment too small.

REMEDY: Install larger service equipment or if two-wire, install three-wire equipment.

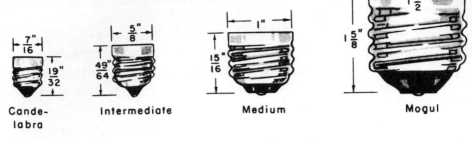

L-3. Common lamp base sizes.

## TYPES OF ELECTRIC LAMPS

Lamps may be grouped into three general classifications:

1. Filament and fluorescent, designed primarily to produce visible light.

2. Lamps designed to generate radiant energy in the infrared region -- heat and drying lamps.

3. Lamps designed to generate specific ultraviolet radiation -- bactericidal and sunlamps.

In this book we are concerned only with lamps designed to produce visible light.

## LAMP BASES, LAMP SHADES

Four lamp-socket sizes are in general use, the candelabra, intermediate, medium and mogul, as shown in Fig. L-3.

The drawings in Fig. L-4 show most of the lamps ordinarily used in the home.

## TEST LAMP YOU CAN MAKE

A handy lamp for locating trouble, checking to see whether wires are live, etc., is shown in Fig. L-5.

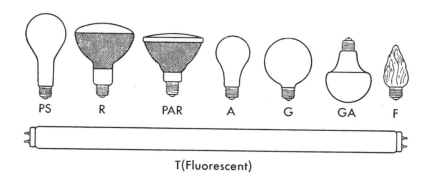

T(Fluorescent)

L-4.   Lamps used in the home: PS-pear shape, R-reflector, PAR-parabolic, A-common lamp bulb, G-globe shape, GA-decorator, F-flame, T-fluorescent tube.

Such a lamp may be made by connecting two well-insulated No. 14 wires about 15 inches long, to a non-metallic, weatherproof lamp socket. After attaching the wires to the socket, about one inch of insulation should be removed from the exposed ends of the wires and the ends taped as shown in the drawing. Screw a lamp of low wattage into the lamp socket, replace the protective guard, and the tester is ready for use.

TAPE

WIRE WITH INSULATION OFF

L-5.   Improvised trouble lamp.

In using such a test lamp to check for live wires, grounds, shorts, open circuits, etc., be sure to stand on a dry board or box, and be sure to keep your hands well back on the insulated portion of the wires.

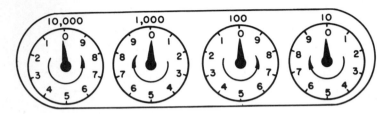

L-6. Electric meter. Arrows indicate direction hands on dials rotate.

## READING ELECTRIC METERS

Electric meters register in kilowatt-hour units. A kilowatt-hour is 1,000 watts in operation for one hour.

Fig. L-6, shows how the four dials look on a typical meter. Arrows indicate the direction the hands rotate.

To take a reading you must read all four dials of the meter. The figures on the dial at the extreme right measure individual kilowatt-hours. Each figure on the second dial from the right shows 10 kilowatt-hours. Each figure on the third dial from the right represents 100 kilowatt-hours. Each figure on the dial at the left represents 1,000 kilowatt-hours.

To fix these values in your mind, remember that the dial at the extreme right is capable of registering 10 kilowatt-hours    The second dial from the right is capable of registering 100 kilowatt-hours. The third dial from the right is capable of registering 1,000 kilowatt-hours. The dial at the left will register 10,000 kilowatt-hours.

In each case, the last figure passed by the hand, and not the nearest, is used in the reading. When the hand

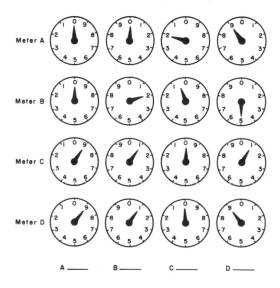

L-7.    Four electric meters, to give you practice in reading the dials.

seems to be right on the number, the dial at the right should be consulted to see whether or not the number has been passed.

In reading a meter, always start with the dial on the right and remember that the pointer on the right dial must make one complete revolution before the indicator on the next dial moves one number.

The kilowatt-hours used in a month are determined by subtracting the reading at the start of the month from the end-of-the-month reading. Before you can figure the cost of the electrical energy used, you must obtain information on rates from the utility company. You will find that the cost per kilowatt-hour goes down as you use more electricity.

As a test of your ability to read a watt-hour meter, try reading the four meters shown in Fig. L-7.

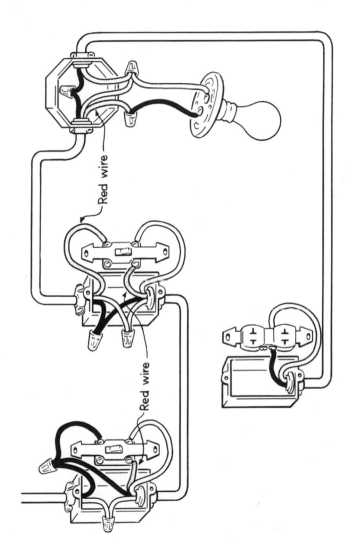

Red wire

Red wire

L-8. Adding outlet and ceiling light beyond both switches. Two 3-way switches are required. When wired as shown, the outlet is always hot. Be sure to keep in mind the fact the black wire leading from the current supply is the hot wire, and the one in which switches are to be installed.

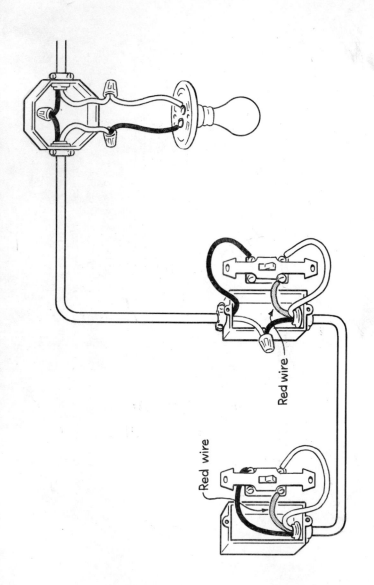

Red wire

Red wire

L-9.  Wiring required to control ceiling light beyond switches,  using two 3-way switches.

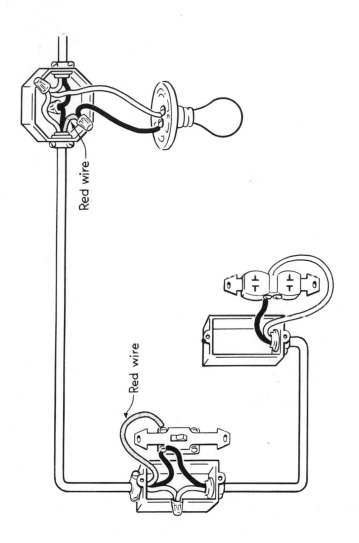

L-10. How to install outlet and switch beyond existing light. The outlet is always hot.

Red wire

Red wire

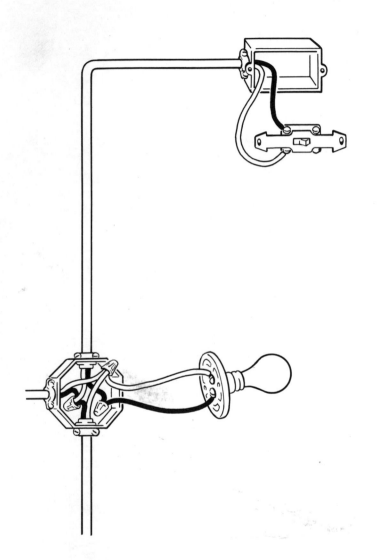

L-11. Using wall switch to control light in middle of run.

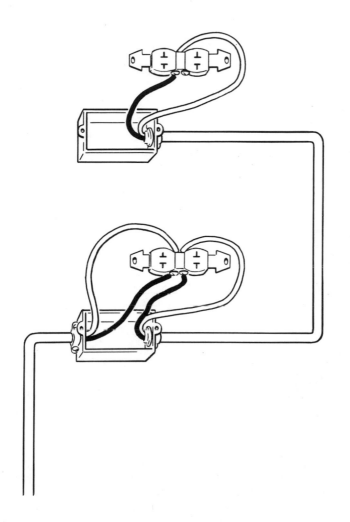

L-12. Adding new convenience outlet beyond present outlet.

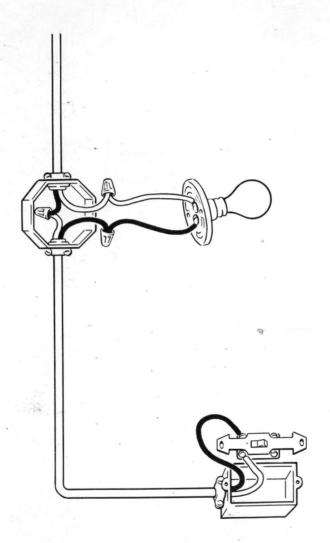

L-13.  Installing wall switch to control light at end of run.

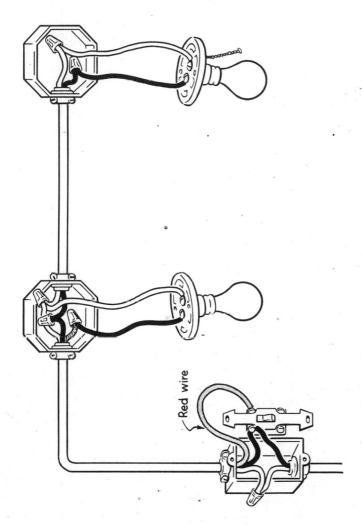

L-14. Wiring two ceiling lights on same line; controlling one with wall switch, other with pull chain.

Red wire

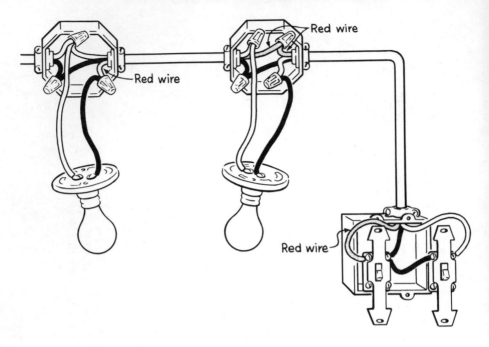

Red wire

Red wire

Red wire

L-15. Adding one new ceiling outlet and two new switch outlets beyond existing outlet.

## ACKNOWLEDGMENTS

The publishers of ALL ABOUT HOUSE WIRING wish to say "thank you very much" to the many individuals and organizations whose splendid co-operation has made this book possible. Particular credit is due:

General Electric Company; Industry Committee on Interior Wiring Design; National Adequate Wiring Bureau; Sears, Roebuck & Company; University of Illinois; Washington Electrification Committee; Westinghouse Electric Corporation; Wiremold Company.

# *Index*